Praise for
The Pepper Effect

Sean Gaillard's ability to connect with individuals in such an uplifting, powerful way in *The Pepper Effect* produces a creative energy and synergy to propel people to tap into their passion, purpose, and positive vibes to elevate together as a collective unit. He's the best lead singer any band member can hope for and a true mentor and friend. It's time to start jammin' with *The Pepper Effect*.

—**Jennifer Burdis,** author of *The EduNinja Mindset:*
11 Habits for Building a Stronger Mind and Body

Like The Beatles, Sean Galliard inspires everyone within his orbit to do and be their best simply by acting naturally. *The Pepper Effect* is for any individual who celebrates the rhapsodic interplay between teaching and learning. I recommend this book to educators, parents, and all others interested in seeing the world from this fabulous perspective. The inspiration you take is equal to the inspiration you make.

—**Brad Spirrison,** senior director, Participate

The Pepper Effect is from the genius of Sean Gaillard, creator of the #CelebrateMonday Twitter phenomenon. Sean takes you on a leadership journey that bases lessons about leading, learning, and life from The Beatles and applies them to every school. This is not just about a day In the life of a school; it is about getting better with a little help from your friends. This is an incredible book from an amazing leader. Whether you are a fan of The Beatles, Beethoven, or Bruno Mars, this book is for you.

—1

‑ of educational leadership,
ersity of Missouri

In his book, *The Pepper Effect*, Sean Gaillard takes readers on a journey into the world of creativity, collaboration, and innovation. Reading this book is an experience. It is an experience that ignites the senses and is sure to inspire and impact every educator who reads it. Through Sean's gift for storytelling, he hearkens back to the fundamentals and core of one of the greatest bands of all time, The Beatles. *The Pepper Effect* reveals the lessons Sean has learned along the way—combined with the artistic synergy of The Beatles—and paints a beautiful picture for how we can apply all of these insights to our own professional practice.

—**Laura Fleming,** author of
Worlds of Making and *Making Great Makerspaces*

The Pepper Effect is a delightful glimpse into the iconic work of The Beatles with inspiring stories of powerful educational leadership and school transformation along the way. Using his passion for music and The Beatles, Sean inspires with a narrative that instantly connects with those of us doing the challenging work of school transformation. *The Pepper Effect* will re-energize your leadership practice and is a must-add to every leader's "set list" of school transformation reads!

—**Randy Ziegenfuss,** superintendent of Salisbury Township School District, Allentown, Pennsylvania, and co-host of *TL Talk Radio Podcast*

Sean is a masterful storyteller. He interweaves the story of The Beatles and the school into an inspiring call to action to do more and be more for all of our students. This is the book that I needed to read. Sean makes the steps to create a collaborative and creative culture seem natural. I am ready to make my school a better place because of his writing.

—**Megan Morgan,** lead support teacher, Davenport City Schools, Iowa

Sean Gaillard's *The Pepper Effect: Tap into the Magic of Creativity, Collaboration, and Innovation* takes the magic of The Beatles and transforms it into a thoughtful, practical guide for stimulating collaboration and community. Gaillard sagely draws upon the wisdom of the band's philosophy and creates a user's manual for living the well-lived life—not only in our professional worlds but in the lives we share with our friends, neighbors, and families.

—**Kenneth Womack,** author of *Maximum Volume: The Life of Beatles Producer George Martin*

The Pepper Effect, by author Sean Gaillard, exudes passion through authentic and compelling stories relating education to The Beatles. Brilliantly composed, this book will capture your heart and inspire you to take courageous steps toward fostering a culture of creativity, collaboration, and innovation. Complete with a plethora of practical ideas and questions for reflection and discussion, you'll be equipped to embrace change and be a positive force of impact on your school culture. *The Pepper Effect* is a masterpiece I'll return to time-and-time again, as each read sparks new insights and makes me thirst for more!

—**Elisabeth Bostwick,** award-winning educator and speaker

The Pepper Effect is perfect parts of inspiration, motivation, and practical strategies that come together to blend beautiful harmonies for the school house. Through the pages of this book, Sean shows us that dedication to a strong vision and collaboration, while ignoring the naysayers, can lead to masterpiece experiences for both students and staff.

—**Beth Houf,** principal of Fulton Middle School, coauthor, *Lead Like a PIRATE: Make School Amazing for your Students and Staff*

Sean has masterfully crafted a literary score that connects the genius of the iconic Beatles' creativity to the innovative mindset schools are beginning to embrace—preparing students to learn unafraid and swing for the fences, exploring critical questions that are effectively transforming the 'schoolhouse' experience.

—**Marlena Gross-Taylor,** EduGladiators, LLC

Sean Gaillard provides a lyrical playbook for all educators with *The Pepper Effect*. He weaves interesting stories with Beatles history and applies the learning with practical strategies that can be implemented tomorrow. They say that you should surround yourself with people smarter than you, and in doing so you are inspired to continuously learn and improve. Sean does this for all of us! The insights he shares are so smart and compelling. *The Pepper Effect* is a must-read for ALL educators!

—**Allyson Apsey,** elementary principal and
author of *The Path to Serendipity*

Of all The Beatles books out there, this is the first I've read that relates the Fab Four's career trajectory to pedagogical pursuits. It's engaging, thoughtful, enlightening, and a joy to read. I'll be implementing Gaillard's ideas this coming fall term!

—**Aaron Krerowicz,** Beatles Scholar and author of *Flip Side Beatles*

The Pepper Effect

Tap into the Magic of Creativity, Collaboration, and Innovation

Sean Gaillard

The Pepper Effect
© 2018 by Sean Gaillard

This book is available at special discounts when purchased in quantity for use as premiums, promotions, fundraisers, or for educational use. For inquiries and details, contact the publisher at books@daveburgessconsulting.com.

Published by Dave Burgess Consulting, Inc.
San Diego, CA
DaveBurgessConsulting.com

Cover Design by Genesis Kohler
Editing and Interior Design by My Writers' Connection

Library of Congress Control Number: 2018944107
Paperback ISBN: 978-1-946444-88-2
Ebook ISBN: 978-1-946444-87-5

First Printing: May 2018

Dedication

This book is dedicated to my real Fab Four:
Deb, Maddie, Emily, and Rachel.

I am the president of your fan club, a
grateful husband and father—always.

Contents

Foreword

by Dr. Jennifer Williams,
educator and thought leader

John Lennon and Paul McCartney truly had an amazing collaboration. They balanced each other out in terms of writing music and lyrics. Sometimes they were eyeball to eyeball writing gems in a hotel room. Sometimes they would write separately, knowing that the other partner could finish a key line or add feedback to make the song better.

—Sean Gaillard, author, principal, pal

Musings. Collaborative thought. Energized work sessions that invite in creative risk taking. Those moments when *what if* ideas land on the "just right" and ready minds needed to move conceptual notions to a place of action. Those times when your words can be spoken free of fear of judgement or commentary and are received in a way that allows them to come to life, to catapult up, and to take flight and soar.

Those are the moments—those professional partnerships—where you enter into a place of trust through mutual vulnerability and can, without any spoken words, just realize, *We are onto something here.*

When you find that type of synergy, you simply seem to know it, or rather, feel it. The harmonies Paul McCartney and John Lennon found in their music, in the process of creation and in friendship, I believe reflect many of the tenets we today seek in education through models of design thinking and inquiry-based learning. Like The Beatles in their offering of powerful ideas centered on imagination, peace, and coming together, we are in a time in education where we similarly are able to lead with empathy and a commitment to shared experience. As educators, we are able to see that sometimes progress toward a goal is messy and oftentimes expansive before we are able to focus and find clarity in details and in meaning. But when built on a unified vision and a constant dedication to what is good and right for students, we can know we are on the right path even if sometimes we find that it is a long and winding one.

If I pause now and think back on times of professional collaboration that have shaped me and my practice, my thoughts are painted with pops of color that remind me of the brilliant uniforms worn by the members of The Beatles on the *Sgt. Pepper's Lonely Hearts Club Band* record cover. The individuals that have been part of those signpost moments in my life were always my tribe, my think tanks, my professional learning network (PLN). And in my work with Sean Gaillard, we will always be able to say, "It started with a tweet."

Let's rewind a bit.

It was a late-winter Saturday morning. I found myself sending out a request for advice. After several years of existing almost exclusively in research and study related to my doctoral work, I realized that my identity as a reader had changed. Days of getting lost in a book or connecting with characters in a story had been replaced by data analysis and sourcing and methodologies. And as a literacy specialist that professed the importance of developing and nurturing a love of reading with students, I knew I needed to find a way back to my reading roots. So with a 140-character message directed at educators I knew only by handles and brief bios, I pushed "send" on my tweet, asking, "Any great suggestions for my new booklist? #goodbooks," and awaited a reply. Within minutes, book ideas started coming my way.

One response came from a principal in North Carolina. The "turnaround principal," as I knew him, that loved to #CelebrateMonday. He reminded us in our PLN that ours was a "noble profession," and he made teachers feel like the rock stars they were by sharing out virtual high-fives to trend the positive. He was the type of person whom probably everyone would claim as "my best friend," which was okay because we all knew that with Sean, there were enough good vibes to go around. Synergy. We all felt it.

And we continue to feel his support and encouragement each day as we go along.

Although they started with a simple tweet, my collaborations with Sean Gaillard—as I know could be said by many others—grew to much, much more. Over the years, we have together and with other "edu-bandmates" pushed against the status quo, leaned into what was good and positive in classrooms and schools, and worked to see the world of education through a lens of whimsy, wonder, and harmony. And as we often say in our group, this is just the beginning.

The Pepper Effect is like meeting a friend for a cup of coffee at a local bookstore or record shop. Sean's invitation to welcome in the magic of creativity and collaboration allows educators to see that a collective story of education is being written by us all. We are part of a masterpiece, an opus, a collection of works . . . a celebration of learning and of stories. Immerse yourself in nostalgia, find comfort in the truth that one can always reinvent and reimagine, and shine a spotlight on those moments that holler to you, "We are onto something here."

Get ready to find your beat in the rhythm of *The Pepper Effect*. Brought to you by my dear pal, the incredible Sean Gaillard.

Guitar Groups
Are on the Way Out

Long before the infinite screams of unabashed fans at sold-out stadiums, before the unbroken string of number one hits, before the iconic performance on *The Ed Sullivan Show*, The Beatles were a small-time bar band from Liverpool, England, seeking the fame and fortune associated with a recording contract.

They were four guys—John, Paul, George, and Pete—doing their best to carve out a space for their sound on the charts. Hustling to secure the backing of any record company, The Beatles faced a slew of rejections. But they were banking on 1962 to be their year. In fact, on New Year's Day, the band walked into Decca Records in London and performed roughly fifteen songs. But they clearly failed to impress because, a month later, another rejection letter arrived. Its curt dismissal, "Guitar groups are on the way out," is surely one of the most shortsighted predictions in pop music history. Undeterred, The Beatles made several bold changes, including hiring a new drummer named Ringo Starr and deliberately focusing on playing original songs. The band members were unwilling to allow their failures to hinder the pursuit of their dreams, and, ultimately, that determination changed the world. The Beatles grew to be the most successful group in music history with more than five hundred million—and still counting—records sold.

Fast forward to 2013 in the media center at Wiley Middle School in Winston-Salem, North Carolina. I was a weary, belabored principal struggling to get through another ponderous faculty meeting. Struggling to salvage yet another negative perception of our school. Struggling not to slip into the abyss of despair with the rest of my team. From my position at the front of the room, I saw some teachers tuning out and searching for any means of escape. Others were dozing off, and a few were using their cell phones on the sly. But I couldn't blame them. I had no perfect, reassuring words, no fun icebreaker to lighten the mood. The meeting was going nowhere fast. I was fairly certain that if I volunteered to do a trust fall, my teachers would walk away and let me smack the ground. To be honest, I'd let me hit the ground, too.

I loved this team of teachers. I loved their resilience, their advocacy for our students, and the journey we had been on to improve our school. I felt like I was failing them just like The Beatles blew that Decca Records audition.

Then this thought crossed my mind: *Decca Records audition? The Beatles? Wait, you love The Beatles, Sean. They have been your favorite band for years. You have all their records, and you are a walking Beatles encyclopedia. When you were an English teacher, you used any excuse to integrate them into a lesson plan. Your classroom proudly displayed Beatles posters and album covers. You were a teacher who connected with his students. So be a principal who connects with his teachers. Why not share with the staff how The Beatles auditioned for Decca Records, got soundly rejected, but survived to become legends?*

Pressing play on this Beatles digression and working up the courage to face a potential mob scene, I talked about the band's decision not to let failure define its path forward. My voice rose in intensity as I shared the now-infamous quote about guitar groups and explained how this little band from one of the most overlooked spots in the British Commonwealth beat the odds and made music history. Heads began nodding as the familiarity of The Beatles broke through the fog. A couple of teachers hummed a few bars from their favorite hits.

Likening The Beatles' failed audition in 1962 to our school turnaround mission served as a bridge for our staff. It was the salve needed to help the team lift its head, keep persevering in the face of false and unfair perceptions of our school, and get back to our vision of inspiring innovative minds. That particular hook helped me not only connect with our team but also stay grounded as a leader. The faculty needed to see their principal as real and relevant and not a robotic leader with canned statements. Speaking about The Beatles from my point of view provided a much-needed support and identifying connection for our faculty as a call to action.

Reflecting on that faculty meeting later, I realized those of us in education can learn a great deal from those four lads from Liverpool. From any perspective, the band's journey and accomplishments are astonishing. From making difficult leadership decisions to learning to collaborate in the face of adversity, The Beatles' narrative offers a plethora of useful and uplifting lessons, many of which can be applied to leading a school.

Sgt. Pepper's Lonely Hearts Club Band, released by The Beatles in 1967 and the basis for this book, provides a template for inspiring the educators inside any schoolhouse to become more positive, innovative, creative, and collaborative. For me, it started with looking at the album's back cover.

What Is *The Pepper Effect?*

When I was a kid, I heard the rumors and hype behind the Paul-is-dead urban legend. It was the one where Paul McCartney died tragically in a car accident, and the surviving Beatles hired a replacement who looked and sounded like Paul McCartney. According to the legend, the band allegedly proceeded to plant all kinds of clues about McCartney's fate on album covers and in backwards song messages to help fans unravel the mystery. Or so the legend says. Even today, it's a fun and silly game to play.

I, for one, scoured the back cover of *Sgt. Pepper*, looking for Paul-is-dead clues, and I came across a randomly placed lyric from one of the album's tracks, "A splendid time is guaranteed for all," in the bottom right-hand corner. It didn't make sense to me, because the back cover of the album displays all of the song lyrics. This particular lyric from "Being for the Benefit of Mr. Kite!" is already listed within the sequence of the album's words. I never understood why it was there. Perhaps it was a message from The Beatles to their listeners about the joy and creativity that was embedded within the tracks of their audio masterpiece.

> A splendid time is guaranteed for all!

"A splendid time is guaranteed for all" is a suitable opening to *The Pepper Effect,* and I believe it's the ideal greeting for everyone entering a schoolhouse. Can you imagine starting a school day with the festive, circus-like nature of that particular song? That positivity is the attitude all schoolhouses must be rooted in as we are in the collective agency for world-changing work.

Now let's point the lens at The Beatles and take an imaginary walk through their recording studio makerspace.

Imagine if EMI Recording Studios (later to be known as Abbey Road Studios) was a gallery where the sonic tapestries created by The Beatles there were mounted and framed for all to see. What images would we see displayed from the *Sgt. Pepper* era? Perhaps we would see Paul McCartney laying down the fluid and melodic bass tracks for "With a Little Help from My Friends" or maybe a photo of George Harrison directing his guest Indian musicians for the ethereal raga drone of "Within You Without You." John Lennon demoing on piano the surreal landscape of "Lucy in the Sky with Diamonds" would make a beautifully framed portrait. Or we could survey the percussive answers of Ringo Starr locked in the lyrical synchronicity of "A Day in the Life" with his drums providing well-timed responses to the ebb and flow of the song.

The image I prefer to envision is the band gathered around a battered piano in the cold, echoing confines of Studio 2. Producer George Martin is in a crisp, pressed dress shirt with a tie swaying in time to the chords being played on the piano. Our Fab Four, no longer in their *A Hard Day's Night* suits and Beatle Boots, are mustachioed and wearing the paisley, crushed velvet of Carnaby Street. A knowing smile is exchanged by the band as they run through a rough tune entitled "In the Life Of." This song, pieced together from separate scraps written by John Lennon and Paul McCartney, will serve as a shining example of the album's majesty, timelessness, and impact.

Proclaimed by many to be the band's most revolutionary era in their recording oeuvre, *Sgt. Pepper's Lonely Hearts Club Band* took the template of pop music and smashed its established standards against a day-glow wall of rebellion. The album signaled a paradigm shift in musical expression. After its June 1, 1967 release, bands would forever embrace or avoid comparisons to this album. The terms "masterpiece," "psychedelic," and "concept album" are freely associated with *Sgt. Pepper*.

Books, tributes, and documentaries fill the space around this album. Its studio innovations alone have served as the basis for endless analysis and discussion. The dated trappings of the Summer of Love are aligned with the release of the album. The final haunting chord of "A Day in the Life" or the album's groundbreaking gatefold cover are freely referenced by Beatles fans and scholars alike.

What I believe is often overlooked in those discussions is the culture of creativity, collaboration, and innovation that helped move the band to that critical place where *Sgt. Pepper* was within their reach. I call this The Pepper Effect. The Beatles harnessed this mindset with the need to do something different with their recorded work. The band was intentional in this progression and very much aware of the studio production race that was happening with prime movers in music such as Brian Wilson, Phil Spector, and Berry Gordy.

The Pepper Effect fueled experimentation within the studio during the recording of their masterpiece. Their collaboration pushed and nudged them to collective new heights and allowed them to embrace risk taking moves, such as adding comb and tissue paper instrumentation on songs like "Lovely Rita" or adding a forty-one-piece orchestra to play what producer George Martin called "a tremendous build-up" for "A Day in the Life."[1]

Moving from our fantasy recording studio to a school, imagine visiting a seventh-grade math class filled with a diverse group of learners. The teacher is coteaching a lesson with the school's media specialist, and they have decided to take a problem-based learning approach to a particular lesson. Students are working in groups inside the library's makerspace. Each group is inspired to provide a creative solution to a complex real-world problem involving application of statistics, probability, and computation. Students are creating meaning

---

1 Hertsgaard, Mark. *A Day in the Life: The Music and Artistry of The Beatles,* Canada: Delacorte Press, 1995.

and visualizing their learning, and their teachers have established a culture that is positive and inviting for all learners.

The Four Cs of education—collaboration, creativity, communication, and critical thinking—are alive and happening in real-time as students are pushing their thinking with intentional purpose. This is not a traditional classroom where students are aligned in rows and a teacher is lecturing. The makerspace has the feel of Studio 2 circa 1967 at EMI Recording Studios. (For more on makerspace, check out Laura Fleming's dynamic and invaluable website: Worlds of Learning at worlds-of-learning.com.)

The Pepper Effect is resonating in dynamic actions among the students in the school. Students are creating their own respective masterpieces with differentiated support and encouragement from their teachers. Teachers and administrators are freely exchanging creative ideas to enhance the school vision. Everyone is included and inspired to innovate. It is almost as if you can hear The Beatles and George Martin nodding in approval at the creativity taking place in the classroom.

The past few paragraphs are not a mere fantasy sequence. These things do take place in schools around the world, and I have been privileged to take part in innovative and creative efforts inspired by The Pepper Effect. My hope is to share my story as a lead learner and educator who happens to use The Beatles as a leadership hook.

> Everyone is included and inspired to innovate.

We will explore in this book the various lessons gleaned from The Pepper Effect and connect them to the schoolhouse. The Beatles inspire us not only with their compelling and timeless music, but also inspire us as educators to take bold, innovative steps in service and support of our students.

Each chapter will begin with a tale from The Beatles' narrative derived from the composition and recording of *Sgt. Pepper's Lonely Hearts Club Band*. As an unabashed music geek, I am calling that section Side 1. It will connect to a real-life application in the schoolhouse, and the real-life application will be called Side 2.

There are a few Interludes along the way, and while they stray from the *Sgt. Pepper* narrative, they are connected to other inspiring threads from The Beatles' story that can also apply to the schoolhouse.

Each chapter will include a Mix Tape for Next Moves and Grooves in your journey to build more creativity, collaboration, and innovation in your school. Mix Tapes were the homemade cassettes you created for a thematic music mood or to simply share music with a friend. Featured at the end of each chapter, the Mix Tape will highlight questions for discussion and reflection as well as possible action steps.

What if schools embraced The Pepper Effect in service and support of all kids? What strides could be made if we fully adopted this mindset? What if teachers embraced the collaborative spirit as The Beatles did in creating their 1967 album masterpiece?

My answer lies within the upcoming pages of this book. I believe that in taking on the creative and collaborative mantle of The Beatles, an entire faculty can transform a school.

Whether you are a teacher, instructional coach, specialist, or administrator, The Pepper Effect is intended for you. There is no need to listen to every song title by The Beatles or have an encyclopedic knowledge of a band that dissolved nearly fifty years ago. I will happily supply the music background for you. If you are passionate about fostering a positive culture of collaboration in your respective schoolhouse, you will most certainly feel at home.

As my father says, "Everybody plays, and everyone is off the bench." As educators, we are all called to lead, motivate, and inspire, regardless of our titles. The Beatles were a truly democratic union, and each member of the band demonstrated leadership in his own way. I'm challenging school faculty teams to follow in The Beatles' footsteps.

As you read this book, I hope you begin to discover other bands and musicians that feed your passion and motivate you to create your own leadership hook for your schoolhouse.

What is the Pepper Effect? The Pepper Effect is best encapsulated in the following four steps:

1. Believe in your vision.
2. Believe in your masterpiece.
3. Believe in your collaborators.
4. Ignore the naysayers.

We will explore each of these steps as we navigate The Beatles' amazing journey and their innovative process of creating *Sgt. Pepper*. My intent is to demonstrate how these steps connect to fostering a positive and innovative culture within the schoolhouse.

The Beatles created and recorded *Sgt. Pepper* without being bound by limits. There was no direct precedent for this album, and the band embraced innovation and courageously embarked upon unchartered territory. A schoolhouse is capable of adopting a similar approach in transforming its vision or a specific instructional practice.

When I walk into a school, I believe each student I see has the potential to be a future innovator. I remind my teacher colleagues that we are the catalyst. We can be The Beatles for our students by filling their world with possibilities and inspiring them to take giant steps.

Our students have much to offer and, with a dash of The Pepper Effect, we just might help them change the world.

The Beatles Had a Principal, and His Name Was George Martin

He was friendly, but schoolteacherly: we had to respect him, but at the same time he gave us the impression that he wasn't stiff—that you could joke with him.

—George Harrison on
Producer George Martin
from *The Beatles Anthology*

———— SIDE 1 ————

It all started with a necktie.

Aiming for a more grandiose angle, one could say the trajectory of twentieth-century popular music shifted, thanks to an impish remark made by a nineteen-year-old George Harrison to producer George Martin in June of 1962.

Harrison was a member of a little-known band from the north of London. This pop quartet had just concluded an audition for the EMI recording label, and Martin was lecturing them about the recording studio standards. And he was one to know. An impeccable professional with a classical music background, Martin was head of the Parlophone label, a small, eccentric subsidiary of the global record giant known as EMI. Still, as young, headstrong musicians, Harrison and his bandmates weren't terribly interested in Martin's insights—and it showed.

When Martin noticed his listless audience, he paused his lecture and gestured for the band to share if there was anything they didn't like about the proceedings.

Without missing a beat, Harrison, the lead guitarist, responded, "Well, for a start, I don't like your tie."[1]

The ice was immediately lifted, and the natural charm of the auditioning band shifted into high gear. Their infectious humor and camaraderie gave George Martin notice. Soon after, he signed the quartet to the Parlophone label. History was made. The Beatles became "the toppermost of the poppermost" in Europe.[2] Two years after that audition, they conquered America, and the world was overrun with Beatlemania.

Fast forward to February 1967. Martin is standing on a conductor's podium attempting to explain to a forty-piece orchestra how to achieve a sound akin to apocalypse during the *Sgt. Pepper* sessions. The Beatles are gathered with family members, friends, and associates for a celebratory recording session for their song "A Day in the Life."

---

1 Womack, Kenneth. *Maximum Volume: The Life of Beatles Producer George Martin, The Early Years, 1926-1966, Chicago:* Kenneth Womack, Chicago Review Press, 2017.

2 The Beatles. *The Beatles Anthology*, San Francisco: Chronicle Books, 2000.

Over the course of five years, Martin's role as producer for The Beatles had evolved from a directorial approach to one of supportive collaborator. As The Beatles grew as songwriters and musicians during this short period of time, Martin grew with them. He became an invaluable and literal sounding board for the band. Merging their imaginative ideas with his trained background in musical composition, scoring, and studio recording proved to be a template for timeless recordings, including "Yesterday," "In My Life," and "Tomorrow Never Knows."

By early 1967, The Beatles had taken pop music through the audio looking glass with their innovations in form and function of the traditional radio-generated hit. Martin proved to be a necessary ingredient in The Beatles' approach to song. His ear was tuned in to their collective ideas, and he was a willing accomplice in their quest for innovation.

The Pepper Effect is the full realization of this collaboration. Martin's production technique is a textbook example for all scholars and musicians of the twentieth-century recording studio. Whether it was attempting to capture the smell of sawdust in John Lennon's carnival jaunt of "Being for the Benefit of Mr. Kite!" or merging the Indian raga sensibility of George Harrison for "Within You Without You," Martin became Merlin concocting his studio alchemy with his four King Arthurs.

——— SIDE 2 ———

As an educator and principal, I often look to Martin for inspiration. I marvel at how he was able to collaborate with and build a foundation with a band that truly changed the course of music. As an unabashed fan of The Beatles, I view Martin's role as producer as my dream job. When I find myself in those despondent times, I often ask myself the question, "What would George do?"

Martin was a professional. He carried himself as the quintessential British gentleman. His passion for music, innovation, and collaboration enhanced his inherent and quiet rebellious streak.

If Martin was a school principal and The Beatles served as his faculty in the school known as Abbey Road Studios, what might Martin do as principal?

My guess is Principal George Martin would be a sincere and positive presence for his teachers and students. He would be open to creative thinking and encourage his school to be a laboratory for big ideas. He might encourage his teachers to "think symphonically" when it comes to designing lessons to engage students in creativity. His office door would be open to all, but I don't think you would see Martin spending much time in his office. He would be out and about, visiting classrooms, coaching teachers, and connecting with students. I see him listening to and inviting crazy ideas to create a school culture where innovation is a mainstay. I see him taking an artisan's approach to leadership and taking great pride in contributing to something positive in the schoolhouse.

Effective principals lead humbly, with students and teachers at the center of their agendas. While working with The Beatles, Martin was in tune with their musical gifts and encouraged them to soar to new heights as a band. Even when The Beatles rejected his suggestion for a sure-fire hit during their early days as a band, he humbly stepped aside and accepted their original composition. Martin did make one key suggestion, telling the band that the Lennon and McCartney original would be served better with a faster tempo. The band agreed to speeding up the song's pace, and, in the end, everyone appreciated how the new sound gelled. After the recording was completed, Martin predicted the song would be a number-one hit. His prophecy turned out to be true when "Please Please Me" did just that.

The Pepper Effect is more than just studio trickery or throwing an edtech tool into a classroom, hoping that it changes students' lives. Collaboration has to be nurtured and encouraged in an environment where creativity can ignite. Martin was able to do that with his steady hand while collaborating with The Beatles and igniting a revolution in music. A principal must also take on the role of lead learner and encourage the same moves in the schoolhouse for teachers in service and support of all kids.

Tuning in to the possibility of ideas in the name of creativity made Martin an effective producer and collaborative for The Beatles. School principals are called to turn a similar dial on the studio mixing board that is the schoolhouse, as educators are faced with the glorious quest of bringing the Four Cs of education to life for students.

> Collaboration has to be nurtured and encouraged in an environment where creativity can ignite.

Martin also naturally displayed a willingness to listen. This gift of being in tune with Lennon, McCartney, Harrison, and Starr in the recording studio was necessary in creating music. He had to hear their ideas and attempt to translate them into a visceral musical reality. His practice of visible listening is worth exploring as a logical extension to fostering The Pepper Effect in the schoolhouse.

Every band has a template for the creative process. These are the pivotal steps taken to either remain inside or outside the proverbial box. Recording a song for a band can take many forms, and the path is not always the same each time. For The Beatles, there was one step they often took along the way in their studio recording. It involved auditioning a new song in the studio for Martin, their producer and sounding board.

There are many photos that capture The Beatles pitching their songs to Martin. Early studio session images usually depict Martin perched on a stool with his head bowed down and his hands placed on his knees. He is often dressed in a crisp white dress shirt adorned with a thin tie dangling in time to the music. John Lennon and Paul McCartney standing on either side of Martin. Their guitars are slung over their shoulders with voices harmonizing. George Harrison may be slightly off to the side picking out lead guitar riffs and studying the chord formations on John and Paul's respective guitars. Ringo Starr is in the background listening intently to the lyrics and perhaps imagining how his future percussive beats will complement the lyrics of "Another Lennon-McCartney Original."

Martin would listen intently to the tune and provide direct feedback to the songwriters. His opinion was highly valued by the band, and they initially viewed him as a kind of schoolteacher. He might have suggested an arrangement idea or technical suggestion. Perhaps Martin was looking for a teachable moment to take the band down a new path in songwriting and recording. Perhaps he was tuning in to an innovative and whimsical idea a songwriter suggested and looking to build upon it.

The Beatles had a gift of being open to the best idea regardless of who shared it. Martin's direct and timely feedback, coupled with the songwriting genius of The Beatles, led each song to embark on a creative journey that would eventually impact generations of listeners. Their collaboration was always rooted in this first step of auditioning a song before recording. It began with the simple act of listening.

When I started my new assignment as principal at Lexington Middle School, I found myself taking a few pages from Martin's playbook as a leader, educator, and collaborator. It is easy for a principal to leap into a school full of vigor and ideas in the name of change and innovation. I made a similar move in my first principal assignment. Thinking I was going to single-handedly save the school with a simple smile and a quote from a well-thumbed book on change leadership, I stumbled hard over my own ego and stubbornness. I am still learning and striving to hit the same universal notes The Beatles did.

For the first two weeks in my new school in Lexington, I made an intentional effort to practice what I call visible listening. This practice takes on many permutations, but the aim is still the same in service and support of kids, teachers, and the school community. Visible listening means visiting classrooms and engaging with students and teachers. It means engaging authentically and being open to learning more about the pulse of the school. It means sitting down with each team member, whether they are students, teachers, or family members, and setting up time for an intentional conversation centered around three simple questions:

- What is great about our school?
- What do we need to work on together to grow our school?
- How can I serve and support you as your principal and lead learner?

I imagine myself as George Martin sitting on that stool in Abbey Road Studios and the teachers as The Beatles. I am listening to their words and music, looking for ways to learn more about our school. I am in tune with those teachable moments and hoping to share what I can with them. We are sketching out plans to build a masterpiece for our students so they can add to the tapestry of our school culture. We are also building the blueprint for our students to create their own respective masterpieces.

During one of these chats with some of my new bandmates, I noticed I was talking too much. My excitement for our collaboration was droning on, and I could sense that I was spiraling into that non-sensical Charlie Brown Teacher Voice. Stopping immediately, I asked them what their dreams were for our time together. The barometer of the conversation changed, and we made real progress on building our collaboration. I am so happy that I took the time to stop my ramblings so I could tune in to the dreams of my colleagues.

Beatles Producer George Martin knew that actively listening to The Beatles was a crucial element in the recording process. Tuning in to his clients provided the necessary foundation for crafting timeless and universal songs that still inspire us today. His simple act of visible listening led to a world-changing musical canon.

The creative and collaborative focus that is The Pepper Effect helped The Beatles release an innovative album that still challenges and motivates. *Sgt. Pepper's Lonely Hearts Club Band* could not have happened with dismissive or rushed listening. More than fifty years after its release, *Sgt. Pepper* still stands as a pinnacle of recording achievement.

Principals and teachers are called to practice visible listening in service and support of students, teachers, and families. Stopping for those intentional pauses and inviting those whom we serve into the collaborative marrow will lead to world-changing music in the schoolhouse. Visible listening is a pivotal move in building the Pepper Effect, and we can adopt that same action to enact bold and creative innovations for our school communities. Visible listening is one of many notes any educator can use to compose a majestic school-house symphony.

———— MAKING YOUR MIX TAPE FOR ———— NEXT MOVES AND GROOVES:

1. **Believe in Your Vision:** What's a vision you have for your school or classroom? How do people not only know that vision, but feel it as well? Does your belief in the vision compel others to support and sustain it?

2. **Believe in Your Masterpiece:** How do you know that your school or classroom is a masterpiece waiting to stand the test of time? What is infinite about the positive imprint you are making?

3. **Believe in Your Collaborators:** Who are some people you would love to collaborate with at your school? What is holding you back from collaborating? Who brings out the best in you as an educator?

4. **Ignore the Naysayers:** How do you ignore naysayers when you're doing something new or taking a professional risk? How do you gain strength from supportive thought partners to overcome the negativity of naysayers?

CHAPTER 2

Walking Away from Candlestick Park and the Same Old Things

That's it. I'm not a Beatle anymore.

—George Harrison after final live
Beatles concert circa 1966

—— SIDE 1 ——

Within a sea of mania, the concluding chords of "Long Tall Sally" resonated throughout a summer evening over Candlestick Park in San Francisco in August 1966. The bandmates leaped from the stage into an armored vehicle, driving away knowing they had just played their last live concert. Putting aside a string of hit albums, number-one singles, and worldwide fame, The Beatles quietly walked away from an established run towards gold-plated success.

It had been a tumultuous tour for The Beatles. The triumph of Beatlemania had been marred with controversy—the inadvertent snubbing of Imelda Marcos in the Philippines, John Lennon's misinterpreted comments on Christianity, and an adversarial press.

A malaise had crept into the band. They were struggling to keep up with the demanding pace of recording, appearances, and simply being The Beatles. Having tasted the fruits of innovative exploration with albums like *Rubber Soul* and *Revolver*, they were anxious to explore and collaborate more in the studio. Live performance had become perfunctory. The screams of fervent fans in packed stadiums drowned out any chance of hearing themselves play, and that adoration did little to fill the void the band was feeling.

The Beatles stood at a vulnerable crossroads in the summer of 1966. They knew that in order to survive, they could not remain on the well-heeled track upon which they were staggering. A radical change of scenery was needed. After Candlestick Park, the band pressed pause on the mania and walked away from being Beatles. John Lennon went to Spain to co-star in a film. Paul McCartney composed a film soundtrack with George Martin. George Harrison traveled to India to study the sitar under the mentorship of Ravi Shankar. Ringo Starr stayed home with his growing family.

—— SIDE 2 ——

Here's an essential question to ponder: Do you walk away from a proven formula for success, wealth, and adulation in order to embrace individual or collective growth?

Or do you dance to the same beat in the schoolhouse and ride out the wave of the next big thing in education?

As educators, we are given many rallying cries to kick aside the status quo and leap headfirst into the sea of change. There are many reasons for this rally cry for transformation within our profession. I will not rewind the tape on the more eloquent tracks laid in order to manifest a transformation in education for our kids, teachers, and families.

How do we encourage one another as educators to walk away from those practices that really aren't producing positive results? How do we invest in so-called best practices that do little to inspire creativity in our kids?

We subscribe to the tried and proven far too often. This mindset leads to a malignant comfort. We cannot afford to stagnate in our quest as educators. Pushing boundaries requires us to be open to The Pepper Effect just as The Beatles were.

I can chant, dance, and weave dazzling words around this, but this movement to change starts with me in the schoolhouse. My words are meaningless unless I provide sincere and sustaining action as a principal and lead learner. It starts with me modeling what I expect. It starts with me putting action behind the belief that I hold for our kids and the future. It starts with me crafting a bridge of support for other teachers wishing to innovate. Simply put, I have to hold myself accountable. Embracing The Pepper Effect can lead to building a culture of collaboration, creativity, and innovation in the schoolhouse.

The Beatles walked away from touring—a successful practice that granted them global fame and a mountain of riches. Touring was their collective bread and butter, and it was a proven formula for making a profit. But they quit touring because they felt that it was preventing them from growing as musicians, among other reasons; furthermore, they quit touring because they were intentional in seeking to innovate

> We subscribe to the tried and proven far too often.

and infuse a paradigm shift in recording techniques. What followed musically from The Beatles continues to resonate and inspire. Following their halt to touring in addition to seeking individual time away from the band, The Beatles produced the double A-sided single "Strawberry Fields Forever" and "Penny Lane." This landmark single was followed by their magnum opus album, *Sgt. Pepper's Lonely Hearts Club Band.*

One could argue this quantum leap in music for The Beatles could not have happened if they had continued in the chaos they were mired in circa 1966. "Strawberry Fields Forever" and "Penny Lane" stand as two of the brightest jewels in The Beatles canon. Both of these songs weave in a tapestry of sound, surrealism, and innovation. A new and exciting direction in music had been forged by the courageous move to walk away from touring.

As a principal, I certainly wish I had a song like "Strawberry Fields Forever" in me to perform for our teachers to inspire global change and innovation. Although I am not a one-man band, I can certainly reach in that creative direction by holding myself accountable to model change—by demonstrating a classroom activity for teachers or providing real-time access to meaningful professional development. I can even flip a faculty meeting in order to model personalized learning. That type of meeting could include desks being ditched with an #EdCamp theme.

Traditionally, principals have been viewed as solitary, detached figures who dole out punishments and quote policies. I have spent my entire time as a principal walking away from that Candlestick Park.

A principal does not have to be a grim reaper. I fight this stereotype daily by embracing my inner Beatles and diving headfirst against convention:

- Instead of calling home with bad news, I surprise students and families with a Principal Positive Phone Call Home.

- Instead of typing up a staid memo, I stir up conversation using Flipgrid with a Weekly Faculty Video Question.

That's one point of view, but all educators are called to walk away from the status quo.

All educators are called to walk away from the status quo.

Most importantly, it is key for any educator to tune in to the gift of collaboration. The Beatles harnessed this gift and brought out the best in each other for the love of music. Tuning in to the gifts of others leads to an authentic synergy in the schoolhouse. Coming together for the common good of serving students is necessary in building a positive school culture.

Here's one riff to play to build that synergy. I call it L.I.S.T.E.N.

L = Look for the gifts of other colleagues in the schoolhouse.

I = Invite colleagues to share those gifts with you.

S = Strategize a plan to build and do something wonderful.

T = Take a risk and commit to do something bold and creative.

E = Enjoy the process of collaborating and camaraderie.

N = Now Make It Happen!

Any educator can do the L.I.S.T.E.N. riff in any setting and at any time. I often do this in the myriad of meetings I attend, as they sometimes evoke much malaise in any profession or organization. In education, we stage meetings for meetings. Take the L.I.S.T.E.N. riff into action at a meeting and flip the negativity into a path for something meaningful.

I was at a meeting and heard a colleague share how she uses Google Drive as a platform to review lesson plans of every elementary teacher in our district. Beyond a simple review, my colleagues use this activity to compel change and start conversations on practice. I was impressed with this feat and saw it as an opportunity to L.I.S.T.E.N. The following day, I reached out to that colleague to learn more about this practice, and now we are collaborating across district on purposeful review and intentional feedback of lesson plans. Our hope is to work together to shift stagnant practices in the classroom and build a supportive environment for teachers to take risks and embrace change. I now have a thought partner to support and empower me to greater heights as an educator.

Never settle for the tried path.

There are many paths we must take to model this change for meaningful action in service and support of our kids in the schoolhouse. A catalyst for change sometimes stares right back at you squarely in the face. It may be hiding in plain sight at a dreaded faculty meeting or required staff development. A simple step back and walkout from the snares of ponderous practice can stimulate new ideas.

Walking away from formulas in education requires courage and vision. Walking towards a new path requires support, modeling, and encouragement. Our schools deserve bold, creative leadership.

What meaningless overused practice will you walk away from as The Beatles did when they stopped touring?

———— MAKING YOUR MIX TAPE FOR ———— NEXT MOVES AND GROOVES:

1 **Believe in Your Vision:** What meaningless practices do you need to avoid in order to protect your vision?

2 **Believe in Your Masterpiece:** What worthwhile practices will you protect to help sustain the drive to do something bold and creative in your school or classroom?

3 **Believe in Your Collaborators:** Do we have the courage as educators to address the pitfalls, mediocrity, and senseless instructional moves? How do we demonstrate belief in our collaborators to call them out when they hit the detours of stagnant teaching practice?

4 **Ignore the Naysayers:** How do you withstand the negative attitudes of colleagues who wish for you to embrace the status quo? How do you rise above the pull to be complacent?

Going Global with The Beatles

CHAPTER 3

—— SIDE 1 ——

"*Om.*"

John Coltrane heard it when he wrapped his saxophone around his legendary "sheets of sound." Michael Bloomfield heard it when he cracked the modal code on his Gibson Les Paul for his song "East-West." The Byrds heard it as they attempted to launch a twelve-string Rickenbacker on "Eight Miles High." Ray Davies might have heard it before all of them one morning in India when he listened to some fishermen chanting on their way to the ocean. These chants served as the basis for The Kinks on "See My Friends."

Ravi Shankar heard it before all of us as his sitar perched on his knee and his fingers danced on the strings, tracing a new raga for an Eastern morning.

George Harrison heard it on the set of "Help!" A scene in an Indian restaurant involving a group of musicians struck a chord within him. These musicians were playing traditional Indian instruments of sitars, tablas, and tambouras. The music felt familiar to the Beatle guitarist, and he quickly picked up a sitar.

That sitar later found itself on "Norwegian Wood," a Lennon-McCartney composition from the 1965 *Rubber Soul* album.

In picking up the sitar, Harrison became more than a musician looking for the right tool for a song or someone indulging in a passing fad. His embrace of the instrument became a lifelong quest for spiritual enlightenment, global understanding, and inner peace. In seeking to learn more about the sitar, Harrison met Ravi Shankar. Shankar was a master of the sitar and became both a musical and spiritual guru for Harrison. This influential friendship served as a powerful catalyst, prompting The Beatles and the rest of the world to look to the East for spiritual meaning.

Pre-*Sgt. Pepper* tracks like "Love You To" and "Tomorrow Never Knows" demonstrated the profound impact India had on the band. There were many influences The Beatles were soaking in during this time, and the Indian impact on the music led to groundbreaking movements in musical expression. "Tomorrow Never Knows" served as a quantum leap for the band with tape loops, sitar, tamboura and Ringo Starr's unforgettable drum breaks. This particular closing song on *Revolver* serves as a powerful hint at the next steps The Beatles were taking in the studio.

The following pages from "Tomorrow Never Knows" in 1966 led towards the roads of "Strawberry Fields Forever" to "Penny Lane" and then to the *Sgt. Pepper* album. Skip forward a few pages on the *Sgt. Pepper* album to Side 2 and its opening mystical drone of "Within You Without You."

Flipping to Side 2 of *Sgt. Pepper* is another jump into hyperspace after an album that takes the listener on a paradigm shift from the onset. "Within You Without You" is essentially Harrison's composition. The song is overt in its Indian influence. Harrison unabashedly peppers the song with sitars, tablas, and the musical lessons he learned from Ravi Shankar. Producer George Martin infuses the song with an orchestral arrangement that deftly blends the musical sensibilities of East and West. Strings drone and harmonize with fluid echoes of sitars and other instrumentation performed by the Asian Music Circle of London. On top of this mini-raga, Harrison echoes the Hindu concept of Maya or illusion and proclaims that love can save the world, much like the deep philosophical truths that would dominate the majority of Harrison's lyrical output with The Beatles and later as a solo artist.

——— SIDE 2 ———

The Beatles leave us with so many education and leadership lessons that do indeed connect in the schoolhouse today. Schools today are fast becoming platforms for students to develop global awareness in an ever-shifting world. The world is becoming a place where we are called to see beyond ourselves, and schools are doing innovative things to inspire students to get in tune with the world.

Imagine George Harrison as a twenty-first-century educator. If he were in the schoolhouse today, my guess is he would stand as a teacher leader for global collaboration. His global awareness and understanding would be a definite gift for any student seeking to develop meaning and action for the world. I can see him leading a Google Hangout on Sustainable Development Goals and collaborating with other educators around the world like Fran Siracusa. Perhaps he would co-present at the International Literacy Association Conference with Jennifer Williams about sincere technology integration for developing nations. Maybe he would be a guest moderator for a #GlobalEdChat with Heather Singmaster on the topic of enhancing students' cultural awareness with the music of India. Perhaps Harrison would collaborate with a global edtech company like Kahoot!, assisting them with strategies to bridge achievement gaps in developing parts of the world.

In this imagined scenario, he might develop meaningful, planned lessons with Cleary Vaughan-Lee of the Global Oneness Project, which could serve as a resource for other teachers learning how to inspire students with broadening world perspective. I can also see him collaborating with Brad Spirrison of Participate on building intentional global awareness strategies through professional development at the school level.

I see Harrison in his classroom encouraging students to take global action for children in war-torn countries like Syria. Perhaps they'd stage a school concert aimed at raising awareness of the tragedies their global brothers and sisters were enduring. It would be reminiscent of "The Concert for Bangladesh," which Harrison organized in 1971, the first true rock charity concert for the flood-ravaged land of its namesake. The concert started as a plea from his friend Ravi Shankar. Harrison and Shankar gathered musicians from all over the world to perform. Ringo Starr, Eric Clapton, Ali Akbar Khan, Billy Preston, Klaus Voorman, and Bob Dylan joined together to make a musical statement. Most importantly, it was a selfless, global action on behalf of those suffering in Bangladesh.

A note from a sitar sent a guitarist from a small Northern England town on a journey of enlightenment that ultimately led to world-changing steps. The Pepper Effect served as a catalyst for musical enlightenment in Harrison's "Within You Without You." It still inspires educators and students to take global action for meaningful change. We are called to tune in to the eternal rhythms and beats of our global neighborhood. Tuning in to the notes and global sounds, as Harrison did, bonds us closer in our humanity and creates universal empathy. We are all invited to join in that global collaborative band in service and support of our schoolhouses.

On another level, The Beatles believed that music could change the world.

A bold statement to leave dangling, but it's true. Their cultural impact on the 1960s and the decades that followed is beyond comprehension. Fashions changed because of the Fab Four. Hair grew longer thanks to John, Paul, George, and Ringo. Their musical statement of love, peace, and understanding helped shape the social consciousness of the 1960s amidst the backdrop of the Civil Rights Movement, the Vietnam War, and counterculture evident in the Hippie movement. But the band's legacy reaches far beyond pop culture and record sales. It left the world with a canon of works that continues to inspire millions to look at the world differently and craft positive changes for it.

A schoolhouse can change the world like The Beatles did.

Consider the fact that education is the catalyst for change in service of our kids. Educators are called to inspire, motivate, and challenge students daily. That's at the core of my being as an educator and principal. When I walk into a schoolhouse, I believe that somewhere in the building is the next Steve Jobs or Frida Kahlo.

This sentiment is something I share relentlessly when I have any chance to speak with students, families, and visitors to our school. I often get a blank stare, but that just fires me up more, and I reiterate the point.

Educating our youth is more than just lesson plans, tests, and school supplies. We are called to do life-changing work. The belief we have for our students that they will be the change to transform the world is a necessary riff for all educators to play.

The Beatles were globally minded and aware of their impact. I contend that they must have sensed that their music was changing the world. As educators, we are called to believe that our impact on students is far reaching and world changing.

If we do not possess that relentless belief for our kids, our work in the schoolhouse is in vain.

Change the world: Teach.

MAKING YOUR MIX TAPE FOR NEXT MOVES AND GROOVES:

1. **Believe in Your Vision:** What are some ways to connect students to having a global awareness?

2. **Believe in Your Masterpiece:** What are some ways to inspire students to engage with global issues and solutions for positive impact?

3. **Believe in Your Collaborators:** How could you collaborate with other educators to connect students to the world?

4. **Ignore the Naysayers:** How will you engage with those who dismiss building global awareness for our students? What will you do to build understanding and keep positive momentum for those who have a limited worldview?

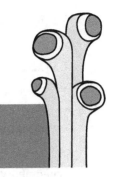

Carving out
"Here Comes the Sun"
Space

Before we go any further, I want to proclaim that I am not in favor of skipping school. As a school leader, it is not my desire for this interlude to serve as a blank check for students and educators to pull a Ferris Bueller and romp off the grid, abandoning all semblance of responsibility.

There is a time and place for whimsical notions to transpire, and we do have to give ourselves permission for the occasional escape. In the last couple of years, I learned about the concept of Whitespace from some educators I connect with on Twitter and Voxer. This is intentional time taken out of the scope and sequence of a packed day for reflection, relaxation, or escape.

As a recovering workaholic principal, I was so uplifted by this idea. I knew I needed a gut check for balance in my life between home and the schoolhouse. Knowing that I needed training wheels to make this happen, I asked our school secretary to hold me accountable. She had access to my calendar, so she plugged in times for me to take some intentional moments away from the grind of the principal's office to recharge. Since I am an unabashed fan of The Beatles, she titled it "White Album" Space as a nod to their classic 1968 double album.

If George Harrison were a principal, his secretary might title scheduled Whitespace as "Here Comes the Sun" Space.

"Here Comes the Sun" was written on a beautiful afternoon in an English Garden circa 1969. This oft-covered and referenced gem from the final studio album of The Beatles was written by Harrison while he skipped a business meeting. The prospect of taking time away outweighed the need to be at the ponderous meeting. In fact, he spent that time in the English garden of a little-known guitarist named Eric Clapton, who also had an acoustic guitar handy for his pal. With that decision to ditch a business meeting, Harrison created a timeless classic for the soundtrack of our lives. "Here Comes the Sun" has been covered by countless artists, and it certainly found its way onto some of my mix tapes over the years.

I cherish "Here Comes the Sun." The tune is one of my go-to anthems for hope, a salve that uplifts each time I listen. There are so many cool moments embedded within that song—George's and Paul's harmonies, Ringo's shifting time signature drum fills, and those hand claps during the bridge. Those supreme hand claps always speak to me as a call to embrace the eternal promise beyond the horizon.

> An intentional move to gather time for renewal can stir inspiration in the most unexpected of ways.

An intentional move to gather time for renewal can stir inspiration in the most unexpected of ways. Educators are a dedicated bunch, and we sometimes default to binding our moves to calendars, meetings, and pacing guides. I have been guilty of forsaking balance and meaningful time with family to meet that district deadline or network at another tedious event. Allowing ourselves the time to break away from the grind is essential to our well-being. And there are so many simple ways to carve out that breathing space:

- Ask a colleague about the last movie she enjoyed.
- Share with students what's on your playlist and ask about theirs.
- Spend time with a favorite song or quote from a life-changing book.
- Follow a few tweets from an inspiring hashtag on Twitter such as #JoyfulLeaders or #CollaborativePD.
- Create something new!
- Spend a few minutes savoring the silence of your thoughts.

Finding that time can be challenging inside a schoolhouse. Our jobs pull on us relentlessly. At times we lose sight of what is meaningful and need a reminder. As educators dedicated to the quest of serving and supporting all students, carving out "Here Comes the Sun" Space is a necessary track upon which we must move. Perhaps taking that time might even lead to the creation of a timeless and universal song like George Harrison's.

CHAPTER 4

Be The Beatles with a Simple Morning Greeting!

——— SIDE 1 ———

Every time I drop the needle on *Sgt. Pepper's Lonely Hearts Club Band*, I get the same rush I had on the first day of kindergarten.

I was five years old, with my Afro Sheened-up hair and a shiny Superman belt buckle, and when I heard Mr. Bennett call my name inside the Analee Avenue School Auditorium, I just knew something amazing was about to happen.

It's the same anticipation I had on my first day as a teacher in that fifth-grade classroom at Saint Gabriel School in Washington, DC. I was writing on the blackboard and thinking to myself, *I am teaching. I am making a difference for the future.*

I felt the same vibe when I was introduced to the first faculty I served as principal at Wiley Magnet Middle School and realized I had been bestowed with the gift of an awesome responsibility for our future.

Every time I hear the opening notes of *Sgt. Pepper*, I feel something wonderful is about to happen. It's that get-ready-you-are-about-to-go-somewhere moment before lifting off in an airplane or making a steep descent on a roller coaster.

It is also the same rush I get on Mondays. I call it my Sgt. Pepper Monday Moment. Why Mondays? Well, why not? Monday is a chance to accelerate the positive in the schoolhouse. Too often, schools and organizations use Mondays as an excuse to be negative. What if we had the same anticipation The Beatles did in the opening bustle of *Sgt. Pepper*? Fans and critics had waited nearly a year for the band to unveil their masterpiece.

What if educators fostered that same anticipation with lessons, activities, and events in the schoolhouse?

It starts with Monday being a positive catalyst for the week.

I started #CelebrateMonday after reading *School Culture Rewired* by Todd Whitaker and Steve Gruenert. I wanted the school where I was first principal to share our story via social media and trend the positive. I wanted each moment in our schoolhouse to be meaningful and positive. I desired for our teachers to share those positives on Twitter. I wanted the anticipation that launches *Sgt. Pepper* to greet every student and teacher in our schoolhouse.

Merging the words "celebrate" and "Monday" in the same phrase was unheard of in common conversation. I was planning to do something via Twitter that had not been done before in relation to education. It was going to be my *Sgt. Pepper* moment.

The premise of #CelebrateMonday is simple: Tweet out the positive things happening in your respective schoolhouse and give a shout-out to someone you admire in education.

Most importantly, the goal with #CelebrateMonday is to uplift, inspire, and transform the day for all in the schoolhouse.

The hashtag has set sail into the Twitterverse and become a trending phenomenon. I am proud of that, but I am most excited that this little love letter to the world has been able to change the conversation on positivity in the schoolhouse.

Like The Beatles allowing the *Sgt. Pepper* album to go on tour for them after their 1966 retirement from touring, #CelebrateMonday travels worldwide and serves as a positivity pivot. It's contagious every Monday morning seeing schools using the hashtag to build that positive anticipation whether it is through Twitter or Instagram. A simple tweet can transform someone's day.

I was even more humbled when I saw Elisabeth Bostwick, an educator in Horsehead, New York, transform #CelebrateMonday in a more personalized way. Bostwick organized an amazing schoolhouse greeting with the local college welcoming her elementary school students as they entered the building. Student athletes were providing high fives, and cheerleaders were shouting, "Celebrate Monday!" to each child.

That beautiful implementation of positivity stayed with me, and I was determined to start it in my third principal assignment at Lexington Middle School.

The opening sounds of *Sgt. Pepper* is meant to the give the listener the feel of being at a live performance. The idea is you're at an imaginary concert where Sgt. Pepper's band is performing. Ambient sounds fill the opening grooves of the album: An orchestra is tuning up and audience voices echo throughout a concert hall. There is a feeling of anticipation and invitation as this fantasy band begins to play.

The Beatles had stopped performing live in 1966 prior to creating *Sgt. Pepper*. The band blissfully retreated to the peaceful confines of the recording studio in pursuit of deeper creativity. The opening track of their new album is a rallying cry of innovation by the alter-ego band they had adopted. It opens its set list with arms extended to the listener. Sgt. Pepper's band is "guaranteed to raise a smile" for the listener. All are invited to come and see the show. The listener is welcomed as being a part of Sgt. Pepper's "lovely audience."

SIDE 2

One day, I was hearing *Sgt. Pepper* resonate in my mind as I was walked into school, and I simply couldn't stop smiling.

I was new to this school community and had entered into a journey as their principal. With this being my third principalship, I was keeping up with a tradition to learn, listen, and visit as I entered the marrow of the schoolhouse. I loved being able to connect with our students, teachers, and families with new and fresh eyes.

It was inspiring seeing one teacher greeting students at the door as they entered our schoolhouse, as this was not a typical morning routine. For various reasons, the teacher had fallen out of love with the profession and was simply biding time, the thrill of connecting with students all but dissolved into a distant memory. That morning, I witnessed an entirely different person than the one I had met at the beginning of my time there, and I marveled at the personal connections being forged.

Earlier, I had spoken with this particular educator in my One-on-One Teacher Time about the importance of having a positive school culture for our kids. We talked about the need to #CelebrateMonday as a way to build a culture that was inviting for all students to feel safe, empowered, and inspired. We discussed the beauty in the simplicity of greeting students with kind words as they entered the schoolhouse. I shared some of the wisdom I had learned from *School Culture Recharged* by Steve Gruenert and Todd Whitaker. It was such an uplifting conversation, and I was thrilled to collaborate with and support this teacher for the upcoming school year.

Seeing this same teacher welcoming students uplifted me even more. I also heard those opening notes of *Sgt. Pepper's Lonely Hearts Club Band* reverberate in my internal turntable and realized this moment was yet another schoolhouse lesson to learn from The Beatles: Welcome all to the masterpiece that is the schoolhouse and make everyone feel valued and invited.

What if every day was a positive opening for a student akin to The Beatles' triumphant fanfare at the beginning of *Sgt. Pepper*? It can happen, and I am thrilled to see how this one teacher served as a positive spark for our schoolhouse.

Those same questions echoed in my mind as I was making a pitch to a community partner for our school. Journey Church is a local neighbor to our school in

> What if every day was a positive opening for a student akin to The Beatles' triumphant fanfare at the beginning of *Sgt. Pepper*?

Lexington, and they devote some of their service to providing simple support for schools in our district. Sometimes it's volunteering in some way or placing a kind note in a teacher's mailbox. I was sharing the idea of #CelebrateMonday to Matt, the youth minister, and his eyes lit up with excitement. I asked him if his team would help in greeting students every Monday like at Elisabeth Bostwick's school. His answer was immediate and affirmative.

Students at Lexington Middle School are now greeted every Monday with high fives, upbeat music, and smiles, all courtesy of our partners at Journey. The front door at Lexington Middle School is not a place for dread or negativity. It is a place for positivity and happiness. Frankly, that should be the norm for every school. We greet students with happiness because we are in the business of igniting the possible for them.

The impact of the sound effects inserted as a fanfare of anticipation on an album cannot be underestimated. A similar fanfare can be created in the schoolhouse. A norm for positive anticipation can be created to uplift all members of the school community. The Pepper Effect can apply to the simple move of having all faculty members welcome students and each other with a sincere smile and fist pump.

_____ MAKING YOUR MIX TAPE FOR _____
NEXT MOVES AND GROOVES:

1. **Believe in Your Vision**: What is the intentional positive moment you are going to create to greet your kids and teammates in the schoolhouse?

2. **Believe in Your Masterpiece**: How do you greet your students each morning? How would you do it differently if you had the time, money, and confidence it would go smoothly?

3. **Believe in Your Collaborators**: What are bold and creative ways to provide daily, relentless belief in your collaborators every morning? How do you greet and welcome your colleagues in a way that is sincere and memorable?

4. **Ignore the Naysayers**: What kind of attitude shift would you like to see at your school? What's something you'd like to change your students' minds about? What are some activities or tasks that your students dread or complain about? How can you change your own attitude to help them view these activities differently?

Making Your Masterpiece in the Schoolhouse

CHAPTER 5

——— SIDE 1 ———

Let's rewind to the fall of 2009. I was a new principal, and that first day on the job truly felt like my first day of school. Ever. I was starting all over, and I had no clue about the joy, angst, and sorrow headed my way.

Everything I had learned in "principal school" was about to go out the window, along with all of the lessons from years of professional reading. Dressed in a fresh, new suit, I walked toward my new school with rapidly eroding confidence. The eternal and optimistic soundtrack that usually spins in my mind was quiet. No visions of what The Beatles would do were coming through to uplift and inspire. It was the loneliest walk I had ever endured. (In principal school, they never told us about all the lonely walks school leaders take.)

Fear gripped me, dancing a demented tango up and down my nervous system. Echoes of negative remarks and blunt questions from friends and colleagues were all I could hear:

"Why that school?"

"The bad kids all go there."

"Those teachers think they run the school."

"Are you sure you want to be a principal there?"

"Why go to the Dark Side? You are a good English teacher. We hate to lose you."

"Well, you got what you wanted. Are you sure you want to do this?"

That last question was my own. I was literally asking myself this question as I moved closer and closer to the front door. Doubt is a paralyzing force. It is also a choice. I was choosing to doubt everything at that moment.

That kind of negativity and worry is a reality many educators face every day. It can also spill over to students and families. Sadly, our schools are often perceived as places to fear and dread. We don't see the good around us. Why is that? Why do we allow negativity to breed around our children? It is educational malpractice when we perceive and promote the negative marrow of the schoolhouse. We cannot tolerate it.

How do we get back to the core of our purpose in the schoolhouse?

The Beatles had horrible gigs and missed opportunities as a band. I am sure that there were times when they did not believe in what they were doing or when they were besieged by uncertainty in their quest for success.

Can you imagine The Beatles being booed off stage? It happened. Can you believe that many esteemed musical experts doubted the band's abilities in print even at the height of Beatlemania? It happened. Can you fathom that The Beatles were laughed at in public, received death threats, and each member left the band at some point? It happened.

There are parallels between the lonely walks experienced by The Beatles and educators.

Perseverance is acceptance of the challenges in life and the endurance it takes to face each one. The Beatles persevered and fueled their drive by believing in their masterpiece.

Believing in your masterpiece means you have a clear vision that the moment you are creating, through whatever act or project, is making a positive impact on others. The Beatles did that with each work they recorded. All of it came from a place of love for music and their audience.

The same can apply to education. Imagine what might happen if we viewed our work in the schoolhouse as artistry. Education does not have to be another set of memos on policy, notes on an agenda, or a worksheet packet. We do not have to give permission to allow the mundane to stifle our fellow educators and the very children we serve and support daily.

——— SIDE 2 ———

Fast forward to January 2012, past countless tears and tribulations. I was standing in my school's media center preparing to announce that our proposal for a federal magnet grant had been rejected. We had navigated the long, complex application process, and we had built a solid, collaborative team in our schoolhouse fueled by a determination to always do what is best, innovative, and uplifting for our students. Trying my best to stay upbeat and smiling, I noticed the entire grant-writing team was standing in front of the faculty. One of the teachers on the team whispered to me, "We heard the bad news, and we are not going to let you stand alone. We got this with you."

Later, our school received a full endorsement from our school board to operate as a magnet school in our district. We could still maintain our vision of a STEAM theme. There would be no funding, but our school was determined to make it happen. In one year, we secured nineteen community partners, doubled our student population to the point where we needed a waiting list, and embedded innovative teaching practices into our classrooms.

During that amazing turnaround, our school team received support and guidance in many different forms. I was especially thankful for my wife and my school colleagues.

Music was also a major source of encouragement. Little elements of songs and albums stitched a tapestry of solace for this principal. Both "Here Comes the Sun" by The Beatles and "Can You Feel It?" by The Jacksons were on constant rotation during car rides into the schoolhouse.

One quote by a certain bass player from Liverpool also became my internal pep talk:

"You just wait."

I whispered these words of wisdom each time I faced a pitfall during my first job as principal. Paul McCartney repeated those words in 1967 as The Beatles were recording the *Sgt. Pepper's Lonely Hearts Club Band* album. Various newspapers were reporting that The Beatles were either breaking up or creatively dried up because it had been almost six months since a new album had been released by the band.

Place this negative mindset in a year when The Beatles had quit live performance after a tumultuous tour plagued by controversy. The double-A-sided single of "Strawberry Fields Forever" and "Penny Lane" was their first 45 release not to reach #1 on the charts. (It only reached a mere #2 on top pop charts instead.) Rumors were abundant as the band retreated to the studio to create their masterpiece.

"You just wait" was Paul's retort to a naysayer-filled media.[1] He knew The Beatles had a major recording ace up their collective sleeves. These three simple words ignited Paul's determination for the band to take a quantum leap forward. The ignorant musings of various naysayers were not going to stifle his momentum. He had a clear vision coupled with supportive bandmates, and they were joined by this dream to record music differently.

McCartney believed in the band's masterpiece. He believed in their collective vision of the album being conceptual in nature, framed by a fantasy concert performed by the band's newly imagined alter egos of Sgt. Pepper's band. He also believed in the musical brotherhood of his collaborators, and he ignored all the critics spinning their negative narratives in the press.

All in all, I would contend that McCartney's quote embodies the ethos of The Pepper Effect. As a principal and lead learner, I have come to see the necessity of building a clear, shared vision for the schoolhouse. It is important to approach all endeavors and journeys in the schoolhouse as having a positive, great, and lasting impact. We want our collective work for education to sustain and resonate as Michelangelo's did with the Sistine Chapel. I think of the #Makerspace work of Laura Fleming and her inspiring students. Laura is an inspiring teacher, librarian, and author based in New Milford, New Jersey. Her work on instilling a vision for makerspace culture has inspired countless students, teachers, and administrators. Laura's students approach creativity with the mindset that their work is meaningful and lasting. I strive to approach my work in the schoolhouse as if I were helping to create a masterpiece of learning for our

---

1 McInnerney, Mike and De Main, Bill *and* Gaar, Gillian G. *Sgt. Pepper at Fifty: The Mood, the Look, the Sound, the Legacy of The Beatles' Great Masterpiece*, New York: Sterling Publishing, 2017.

students. (Check out her "Worlds of Making" website for more inspiration: worldsofmaking.com.)

Education is a collaborative and joyful journey. Love your collaborators and demonstrate your belief in them. I have been blessed with many colleagues who believed in my impossible dreams, and I am called to do the same for the teachers I serve. My hope is that same belief is transferred to our students. Belief is the ignition for inspiration and the foundation for dreams. All schoolhouses must invite that belief for our educators and students.

> Belief is the ignition for inspiration and the foundation for dreams.

The persistent beat of the naysayers will never diminish. If that negative beat was heeded by the great innovators and creators of our time, imagine the tragic gaps we would gaze upon in the distance. Think of a world without the impact of Martin Luther King Jr. or Malala Yousafzai. Imagine a world without the timeless and universal scope of The Beatles. We would not have The Pepper Effect, which has endured as a wheelhouse for lasting innovation.

John, Paul, George, and Ringo left us with a monumental legacy. Their impact still resonates and inspires. This little bar band from Liverpool changed the world. For educators, we are called to create new notes and sounds to change the world in the schoolhouse, just as The Beatles did with *Sgt. Pepper's Lonely Hearts Club Band.*

What masterpiece is the world waiting for you to create?

MAKING YOUR MIX TAPE FOR _____ NEXT MOVES AND GROOVES:

1. **Believe in Your Vision:** How can you inspire students and colleagues to believe in the work they are doing?

2. **Believe in Your Masterpiece:** Start a Masterpiece Challenge in your classroom or for the next faculty meeting. Ask students and colleagues to share one thing they created or started in the schoolhouse or classroom that they believe stands as a masterpiece.

3. **Believe in Your Collaborators:** During those challenging times we face as educators, we have all the more reason to verbalize our belief in one another. Host a Twitter chat with your school's hashtag to boast one another's accomplishments. Create a brag board in a central location where praise can be shared for teacher colleagues.

4. **Ignore the Naysayers:** As Paul McCartney thumbed his nose at critics with the "You Just Wait" statement, how about doing the same with colleagues? When a negative statement comes up from an outside source (I hate to say it, but sometimes there are folks in the schoolhouse who don't believe), retort back with a "You Just Wait."

CHAPTER 6

The Album on Tour: Sustaining the Masterpiece in the Schoolhouse

—— SIDE 1 ——

"The album would go on tour."

That was one idea The Beatles had in recording *Sgt. Pepper's Lonely Hearts Club Band*. Beleaguered by the prison of Beatlemania and touring, the band had quietly ceased live performance. This unanimous decision by The Beatles proved to be the jailbreak needed to embrace freedom in musical innovation. Recording *Sgt. Pepper* was rife with a hodgepodge of conceptual ideas integrated by The Beatles to savor the innovation they were exploring in the recording studio.

Imagine these statements being tossed around Studio 2 of EMI Recording Studios as The Beatles were dreaming their vision into reality:

- "Let's not be The Beatles on this track. We're the Sgt. Pepper band. What would *they* sound like?"
- "There will be no pause between each song on the record."
- "How about comb and tissue paper as a sound effect?"

- "Those twenty-four empty bars need to be a giant orgasm of sound."
- "Surely we can add an orchestral arrangement on top of these Indian instruments."
- "We can add animal noises at the end of the track."
- "Let's toss on a sound that only dogs can hear."

No idea was dismissed with derision. Creative risk taking was the norm. The band believed in full unity. All four Beatles had to vote in favor for a major decision to progress. Deciding not to tour was akin to career and financial ruin, but everyone raised their hands in full favor. The mindset was for their new album to go on tour instead of them.

What a grand and splendid tour for Sgt. Pepper and his Lonely Hearts Club Band! Upon first release in 1967, the album sat comfortably at number one on both the U.S. and U.K. pop charts. Within the following year, *Sgt. Pepper* earned Grammy Awards for Album of the Year and Best Contemporary Album. More than ten million copies of the album have been sold, and the impact is still resonating. Upon the release of the Fiftieth Anniversary Editions in 2017 of the *Sgt. Pepper* album, it debuted again at number one on the U.K. album chart. In the United States, our military band leader reached number three on the Hit Parade.

The Pepper Effect of The Beatles in 1967 has insured that the album will infinitely echo as a timeless and universal work. A masterpiece was forged with collaboration, creativity, and risk-taking serving as a template for the band.

——— SIDE 2 ———

Imagine the following being shared in the schoolhouse:

- Let's take a different approach to our usual problem-solving strategy.
- Status quo is not welcome here. Why don't we dream big today instead of sticking to the regular faculty meeting agenda?
- We are going to apply the EdCamp mindset to all of our math classes this week!
- How about we see what happens if we pair our art and science teachers together for an upcoming unit on force and motion?

None of these statements are far-fetched and can serve students to reach new heights of deeper thinking and creativity.

This type of thinking is vital to pushing against the grain of the status quo. Even more crucial is the response to these statements. I have learned that grand statements about innovation are meaningful if there is an affirmative response. In other words, someone has to say, "Yes."

That yes must then be followed with dynamic, collaborative action.

I love finding bandmates who are willing to go along with those seemingly crazy dreams. No dream is crazy in the schoolhouse when serving a purpose to ignite thought and creativity for our kids. Sometimes it takes finding a willing bandmate who is eager to embrace the random and the whimsical.

Dig this example:

When I first became principal at Lexington Middle School, I noticed an open area where rows of decrepit computers were gathered. It was an open computer lab, but the space was not only an antiquated eyesore, it was not being used at all. I knew something extraordinary had to be done to fix that sad little corner of our school.

I found a willing community partner and a teacher colleague, and we started brainstorming. We quickly realized students were going to be our best source of ideas on how to transform that space. I randomly gathered a group of students, showed them the space, and asked them to help me give it a makeover. We all stood there in that empty space (by that time, I'd removed the old computers), students and teachers together, dreaming out loud. We tossed out ideas and jotted them down on a nearby whiteboard.

The students had all kinds of suggestions. They wanted a space where they could be creative and share ideas. It was important to them that the space was not a regular classroom. It had to be special and different. Their excitement and energy were clear and infectious. We even kicked around the idea of teleportation and time travel for this space. Nothing was left off the table.

Later, I came across a couple of teachers and felt the need to share with them the ideas our students generated. They were energized by the student synergy and took steps to create a collaborative, flexible learning space to promote student voice.

This is the same abandon The Beatles had when creating *Sgt. Pepper*. There was no template for the creation of their masterpiece. They had a vision and will to make it into a reality.

The schoolhouse is the marrow for future masterpieces in the eyes of our children. As educators, we have the same notes to tune into as we approach teaching and learning. Our work as educators is not simply designed to be a mere job. It is a calling to serve as a catalyst for future masterpieces from our students. This is a tall, noble order for all teachers, but if we collectively build an approach that is positive and proactive, then we can sustain The Pepper Effect in the schoolhouse.

As a principal and lead learner, I used to think that sustainability was a cute buzz word to dazzle a school improvement plan or sprinkle on a deadline-driven report. I do not mean to dismiss the importance of sustainability when it comes to building an instructional framework or physical infrastructure in the schoolhouse. Sustainability is sound leadership and remains a necessity when making decisions in any educator's role, regardless of title.

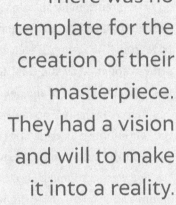

There was no template for the creation of their masterpiece. They had a vision and will to make it into a reality.

By taking on The Pepper Effect in the schoolhouse, sustainability is viewed in the road ahead for our kids and the impact we have on them. In turn, our students all have the potential to create a lasting impact in our world. Part of our varied role as educators is to be in tune with that as we help them forge a path in embracing the possibilities for the future.

When I walk into any schoolhouse, I often think that somewhere there is a student who will solve a global problem or create a positive innovation for future generations. If that student is not in the building, then perhaps there is a student who will be the mother, father, grandmother, or grandfather of that person who will do something world-changing.

Sustaining that mindset is found in so many creative and innovative approaches from ditching desks to creating a more flexible learning environment. Embedding time for students to create in a makerspace or pursue a passion project is another way to sustain that masterpiece in the schoolhouse. Giving teachers time and support to collaborate on building innovative and uplifting learning experiences is another key note to hit in building sustainability. Placing all students in the center of a unifying, positive culture, The Pepper Effect can prove to be a transformative key for the schoolhouse.

We intentionally sustain the masterpiece in the schoolhouse with the belief that all of our students will make a positive impact. Taking a page from The Pepper Effect, a schoolhouse has the ability to have that same resonance as the final forty-five-second E-major piano chord that signals the end of the *Sgt. Pepper* album with "A Day in the Life."

Believing that we do have a resonance is key to all of our moves in the schoolhouse as educators. The classroom is the canvas on which we paint the colors that will shade a legacy for our students.

Sgt. Pepper's Lonely Hearts Club Band is still on a world tour. The album still inspires and delights as an imaginary band loosely resembling The Beatles performs a fantasy concert. The set list is filled with all kinds of musical genres and sound pictures. For the past fifty years, a masterpiece has etched its way into our collective soundtrack. We can aspire to that same level of masterpiece in the schoolhouse as educators collaborating, creating, and dreaming in service and support of our students.

We are in that schoolhouse band, and everyone has a significant part to play—weaving notes, chords, and melodies that inspire students to do great things.

Are you ready to join the schoolhouse band?

Of course you are! You have a beautiful part that will inspire countless students to dance to a stellar beat of goodness.

MAKING YOUR MIX TAPE FOR NEXT MOVES AND GROOVES:

1. **Believe in Your Vision:** How do you leverage and influence others to promote your vision? What does it take to build trust in others to create synergy?

2. **Believe in Your Masterpiece**: We are artists in education, and our work will stand the test of time as we continue to impact the future. How can you flip the mundane into artistry that uplifts a school or classroom?

3. **Believe in Your Collaborators**: Your faculty colleagues and students are your band. Be the president of your schoolhouse band's fan club and champion the collective efforts! Scream like those early fans of The Beatles did. Create your own Beatlemania in your schoolhouse and support your colleagues unapologetically. Delve into the power of the shout-out and tweet out those nods to your students and colleagues.

4. **Ignore the Naysayers**: Why is it important to drown out the negatives in a school or classroom? How do you distinguish critical feedback from naysaying? How can you create value in promoting the positive things happening in your school or classroom? How can others be inspired to do the same?

I Thought It Was You Three: Adding Praise and Thanks to the Schoolhouse

In our pursuit of creating world-changing symphonies in the schoolhouse, it's easy to forget the power of simple praise and thanks. We have the obligatory days of recognition in Teacher Appreciation Day or Secretary's Day. Sometimes those moments seem forced when we attempt to celebrate our colleagues and friends in the noble profession of education.

I realized early in my career as a school administrator that it was my role to be cheerleader and fan club president to the teachers and staff members I served. Unfortunately, I had no control over pay raises, bonuses, or vacation days, but I did have total control over the sincerity of my interactions with our team.

I learned this lesson from the first principal I served under as an assistant. Mrs. Brooks taught me the value of putting praise into action. She would draft a weekly memo for the staff in which she made a point to thank specific individuals for a job well done. Her time in the hallways and classrooms was always filtered with audible words of gratitude and encouragement for students, teachers, and staff members. Her actions made such a tremendous impact on my personal and professional life.

Teachers traverse many challenges, and the days are not always easy. I desired to give our teachers more than just a cold pat on the back. I wanted to give authentic appreciation in vocal, unabashed praise. I wanted to take a page from my old college band days and share a gratitude tactic. I play rudimentary rhythm guitar, and I had the privilege of playing in a few pick-up bands in college. My college band days were nowhere near successful, and lineups were never consistent. In one band, The Skydogs, if a member did something unexpectedly cool or even hit the correct note, one of us would issue the compliment, "Man, you are making it happen!" "Making It Happen" became a rally cry of sorts and served as high praise in our little band.

I decided to share that sentiment with our staff members. Every faculty meeting would begin with a section called "Praise and Thanks for Making It Happen." In my morning memo blog posts, I would begin with shout-outs of "Praise and Thanks." When appearing on the loudspeaker for morning announcements, I would share shout-outs of positive things happening thanks to our students and teachers. Any time we gathered as a school community, I made a point of sharing specific words of gratitude.

In a schoolhouse, it is vital for the kids and adults to hear sincere words of kindness.

People, in general, need to hear that they are headed in the right direction. In a schoolhouse, it is vital for the kids and adults to hear sincere words of kindness. When individuals do not have a visceral sense of gratitude, there is the risk that the culture of the schoolhouse will shift downward.

Culture truly matters if it is rooted in vision, trust, and relationships. Educators will leave a school or district if support is not there, and when this happens, it's the students who lose.

Ringo Starr left The Beatles at one point. His departure was unexpected. He was willing to leave the comfort of the band's stratospheric success, all due to one thing—the absence of love.

My favorite track on the 1968 eponymous album by The Beatles (now affectionately known as "The White Album" due to its blanched jacket cover) is "Dear Prudence." It is a haunting song written during the band's sojourn in India studying transcendental meditation. The song has so many incredible elements embedded within it, ranging from John Lennon's emphatic vocal performance, Paul McCartney's supportive, melodic bass lines and George Harrison's searing bursts of lead guitar. The song is buttressed by a firm backbeat performed by Paul McCartney.

Wait. Paul McCartney on drums? Where was Ringo?

Believing that his percussion skills were not making a significant contribution, he had decided to leave. Adding to this sudden break was the fact that Ringo was feeling like he did not belong in the band. Ringo assumed that John, Paul, and George had formed a closer alliance and he was tagging along as an uninvited outsider.

Ringo decided to announce his decision to leave The Beatles individually to each member of the band. His first visit was to John. Ringo framed his decision around the fact that he felt his drumming was below average and the other three had formed a stronger bond without him included in the mix. John's response to his band mate was, "I thought it was you three!"

His next stop was Paul. Ringo shared the exact same sentiment about leaving, and without missing a beat, Paul said, "I thought it was you three!"

Perhaps fed up by the identical responses, Ringo did not bother meeting with George. The band carried on without him during "The White Album" Sessions. Two songs were recorded with Paul filling in on drums. Feeling bereft without their musical brother, telegrams of praise were sent to Ringo asking him to "come home."

Convinced that the band truly did love him, Ringo returned to Abbey Road Studios to rejoin The Beatles and finish recording "The White Album." Upon his arrival, Ringo found his drum kit bedecked in flowers. They retreated to a smaller studio space to record "Yer Blues," a raw, bluesy number, with the four bandmates locking musical arms.

Taking intentional time to praise and thank the ones we love is a necessary stop along our collective journeys in life. The schoolhouse must be a platform for praise and gratitude when it comes to connecting with our students, educator colleagues, and families. As an educator, I am certain we all have felt Ringo's White Album Moments of Despair. We have been through moments where we don't know if our work as an educator is making a ripple of resonance. We may have been wordless when it came to contributing to those positive nods and words to the faces we encountered in the schoolhouse.

Applying the lesson of gratitude to our daily steps in the schoolhouse is transformational for school culture. We do have to remember that praise must come from a sincere place when serving our students and one another in the schoolhouse. Praise cannot be automated and has to be tied to specific actions. It rolls even better when that praise is tied to the vision and mission of the schoolhouse.

MAKING YOUR MIX TAPE FOR NEXT MOVES AND GROOVES:

There are many tunes to add to the set list of praise in the schoolhouse. Transform someone's day and add value to the schoolhouse with some of these examples:

- Write a handwritten note of praise and thanks.

- Create a daily or weekly blog devoted to schoolhouse heroes.

- Join in the positive Twitter shout-out hashtags like #CelebrateMonday or #JoyfulLeaders and tweet out the positives in your schoolhouse community.

- Share a simple word of gratitude to someone in person.

- Create your own school hashtag intended solely for the purpose of promoting the positives in your schoolhouse.

- Flip a faculty meeting or classroom activity into a time for unabashed praise.

CHAPTER 7

Be The Beatles and
Shed the Status Quo

——— SIDE 1 ———

I am addicted to positivity.

It's true. I thrive on the fix of positivity in the schoolhouse. There is joy in the buzz of a teachable moment. I love seeing those light-bulb moments in students and teachers alike. I love being immersed in the teaching and learning experience. Any excuse to be a part in some way of a positive moment is the fuel that keeps me thriving as an educator.

When we embrace the positive, a different kind of magic happens. There is a certain synergy that occurs when the vision, mission, and people in a schoolhouse blend together. When all of the notes blend together in harmony. All of the challenges and pitfalls that came before the moment dissipate.

We have standards and mandates to meet, deadlines to face, and crucial conversations to endure. Education is a marathon filled with peaks and valleys. When we can transcend the mundane expectations to settle for mediocrity in the schoolhouse, that is when those moments can have a lasting impact.

I believe that the world is essentially a good place. When I encounter a student, teacher or family member, I default to the key of assuming positive intent.

For some educators, we simply share a building space and a master schedule. The schoolhouse is not a home. It is a place where we punch a clock, grading papers and answering memos. We accept the status quo and blind ourselves to the potential symphony that lies in the schoolhouse.

We have heard the tried and true approach to building collaboration among teachers. How many of you have endured the trust falls and same motivational YouTube Videos at the beginning of the school year. I am guilty as a principal of pulling together half-baked icebreakers in an attempt to build community. I was holding back my passion for our pursuit to serve, inspire, and support students. I was allowing fear to grip my being. Truth be told, I wanted to be the "Nice Guy" Principal who simply left teachers alone and abbreviated meetings in order to gain good standing on district-level surveys.

—— SIDE 2 ——

It was not until the failure of our school to secure a federal magnet grant that I realized my approach was all wrong. I had to get back to my passion. I had to "Get Back" like The Beatles did. I wanted to be in a band in our schoolhouse. I wanted us to follow our passions, innovate, dazzle, and create.

It is very similar to what Paul McCartney did when he pitched a fresh approach to the band. He challenged his bandmates not to be themselves. The stagnation of being a simple pop band delivering obligatory, staid hits was something McCartney urged his band to stray away from. They had to leave that well-worn, comfortable path. Simply put, The Beatles had to stop being The Beatles. His idea of his bandmates becoming the Sgt. Pepper Lonely Hearts Club Band stands as one of the most innovative moves the band made. They shed their image in order to free themselves to be bold in their artistic creations. This break gave them the freedom to experiment in new ways, such as adding exotic instruments, key changes, and a sound that only dogs could hear.

I began to share more of my passions and encouraged colleagues to do the same. I was determined not to be chained to the desk in my office. Staying in the office and pushing documents was the typical move of a principal. I was empowered to be more visible and take an active part in professional learning teams and connecting with students more. Any time I could, I would jump into a classroom and simply be in the moment. It was important to model this reinvention as principal and be like The Beatles.

No one can be a solo act in the schoolhouse. I remember encouraging our leadership team to literally take on a new persona to model this approach for teachers at the beginning of the school year. It was a dramatic risk to open the school year in a different tone. The beginning of any school year is a make-or-break event. Start off in the wrong key, and the damage will haunt and negatively shape the culture for the entire year. Begin with an intentional and creative note, and it can spread a legacy of positivity for years to come.

> No one can be a solo act in the schoolhouse.

We decided that we would hold our opening faculty meeting in a different way. Instead of the typical overture of introductions, new policies, and forgotten icebreakers, we showed up in costume as a personal favorite innovator from history. One teammate chose Amelia Earhart. Another colleague selected Vincent Van Gogh. I chose John Lennon. Our goal was to set a special tone for our team of teachers and send the message that we were all embarking on a bold journey of inspiring innovation in our students.

Taking on the physical guise of those historical innovators freed us to have the courage to share our big dreams. It allowed us to be creative and whimsical. Most importantly, it established a positive culture for the challenging year ahead of us.

John, Paul, George, and Ringo adopted the mantle of this imaginary band for *Sgt. Pepper*. Ringo even adopted a different name for one song on the album. He was Billy Shears singing about the joys of friendship on "With a Little Help from My Friends." Taking on a new skin permitted a new perspective of innovation for the band. It was a freeing experience for the band to go beyond the caricature they had become.

Taking on a more innovative approach does lead to more positive experiences. It can also fuel and inspire other educators to even greater heights. When we have that kind of positivity, it will ripple across to our students. I saw so many incredible things as the result of the leadership team taking on the guise of historical innovators. Later that year, I saw a plethora of innovative approaches take place:

- A classroom transformed into an immersive World War I battlefield
- A science teacher who decided to address each student as a scientist, researcher, or astronaut
- An integrated unit where four different content teachers decided to combine their standards to teach ancient Greece to an entire sixth-grade team

We have to embrace the boundless horizon and accept its rightful place in the schoolhouse. As The Beatles pushed against the prickly grains of the status quo, we are called to do the same. Be The Beatles and jump into innovation with arms opened wide. Our kids need that spark of creativity, and the world needs your symphony. Time to play your notes and change the world. Be The Beatles.

MAKING YOUR MIX TAPE FOR NEXT MOVES AND GROOVES:

1. **Believe in Your Vision:** How do you define positivity? What does that look like in a school?

2. **Believe in Your Masterpiece:** What is a creative next step to take to ignite a bold and innovative learning experience in your classroom? How can you extend that experience throughout the school?

3. **Believe in Your Collaborators:** For your next faculty meeting, illuminate the positive in your colleagues by listing the personal talents or gifts each possesses that add value to the schoolhouse. Create a giant list of the positive qualities evident in each individual faculty member and plan a way to harness those gifts in service of your kids.

4. **Ignore the Naysayers:** Establish a Positivity Partner who will help you detach yourself from the temptation to amplify the negativity. For example, I have one of our secretaries remind me with the following statement: "Remember your purpose for our school. Now, breathe." It helps to have that Positivity Partner to be that intentional and direct.

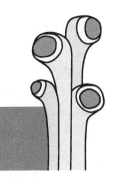

Interlude

A Beatles Reunion: Making the Impossible Possible in the Schoolhouse

Seeing a contemporary picture of Paul, George, and Ringo nestled in a 1995 *Newsweek* cover story on The Beatles reunion stirred a feeling of both wearied disbelief and a shot of optimistic reality. I remember saying to myself at stage-whispered volume, "This is going to happen." My memory wanders backward to my childhood as a Beatles fan, growing up gangly and awkward in an MTV world.

I am, in essence, a second-generation fan of The Beatles. Born after the screams of their American debut on *The Ed Sullivan Show*, I missed the mania. I grew up hearing the echoes of hysteria for the likes of Shaun Cassidy, Menudo, and Duran Duran. While my friends were listening to what was airing on MTV in the 1980s, I was holding my ear up to my clock radio during the late night "Beatles A-Z" Marathon on the local rock station.

It was rare finding kindred spirits who loved The Beatles as much as I did in suburban North Carolina. I faced my share of ridicule in front of peers for not listening to the right kind of music. Whenever I found a classmate who knew the difference between "Yellow Submarine" and "Hey Jude," we became instant friends.

I remember regretting not being around for The Beatles during their heyday. I was always hoping to bump into a time machine that would take me back to a pivotal moment in Beatles history, such as their Shea Stadium Concert. I imagined myself on the rooftop during a cold London afternoon during their final performance as a band harmonizing on "Get Back."

My pastime as a child was jotting set lists for imagined Beatles Reunion Concerts. I remember sitting in front of the television one summer afternoon in 1985 for the Live Aid Concert because of a rumor of a Beatles reunion. It never happened. Paul McCartney appeared at the end and performed "Let It Be." His microphone infamously went off, and his vocal was lost on live television.

I persevered in the hope that the band would reunite. Their negative split in 1970 was filled with animosity and lawsuits. Both John Lennon and Paul McCartney used various songs to bitterly communicate their feelings over their dissolution as bandmates. Any hope of the four reuniting was cruelly and finally dashed with the senseless murder of John Lennon.

In the aftermath of his death, the three surviving members either downplayed or mused upon the possibility of a reunion. I remember clipping quotes from the newspaper if I ever came across a bulletin or a quote on this event. Of course, I fantasized that the band would call upon yours truly to sit in with them. My stubby fingers and rudimentary rhythm guitar prowess would be what a reunited Beatles would need.

I stubbornly held out hope for a reunion. A feeling of joy overwhelmed me as I excitedly thumbed through that *Newsweek* magazine article. The Beatles were reuniting! I remember filling each staff mailbox with a news clipping on the band's reunion in the faculty lounge. My teacher colleagues were used to my passion for music, especially The Beatles. There were understanding glances, but no one joined in the celebration. Looking back, I might have also spent class time rambling about this event. I remember flipping that moment into an activity for students to share an event that they were eagerly anticipating. My students did understand my passion for The Beatles, although it may have had something to do with the Beatles posters covering the classroom walls!

During that fall of 1995, I was knee-deep in the second wave of Beatlemania getting ready to hit the airwaves. Adding to the reunion fever was that the surviving Beatles had collaborated on an upcoming documentary titled *The Beatles Anthology*. A three-volume set of accompanying music was also on the way with previously unreleased outtakes, alternate versions, and two new songs.

As an unabashed Beatles fan, I was near hysterics in anticipation over the notion that the surviving Beatles were reuniting. My recurring dream of a Beatles Reunion was actually going to happen. I did not have to deal with the coy avoidance of the subject from the surviving Beatles anymore. What made this reunion even more poignant was that Paul McCartney, George Harrison, and Ringo Starr ignited their collaboration with John Lennon. They entered the recording studio again with the collective premise that their friend, senselessly murdered by a deranged fan's torrent of gunfire, had slipped out for cup of tea and entrusted a couple of demos for them to finish.

Paul McCartney again devised a premise to help his bandmates create the impossible. Remember that he had a done a similar move when the band was recording *Sgt. Pepper* in 1967. This is The Pepper Effect in full force. Stepping aside from the hype of a band reunion that fans were clamoring for over the previous twenty-five years, The Beatles believed in their vision and each other as collaborators. Most

The Beatles believed in their vision and each other as collaborators.

importantly, they believed in the lasting impact of their fallen friend and bandmate. Creating a proactive scenario helped the band to innovate and persevere through the lasting grief of losing a friend. It also allowed them to overcome the gargantuan hype of a Beatles reunion that had pestered them for over a generation.

The reunited Beatles were able to add lyrics, vocals, and musical accompaniment to an unfinished demo recording by John Lennon titled "Free as a Bird." Another Lennon demo recording was finished, and the band added their musical stylings to it. That song was called "Real Love." Both songs were global smashes and fueled a renaissance for The Beatles at the twilight of the twentieth century.

Considering that the band was able to put aside years of legal and personal battles fueled by a bitter dissolution and enter the studio again with a fresh creative approach is astounding. Adding to the improbability of this scenario was that they were able to reunite with input from a deceased friend. John Lennon's demos of "Free as a Bird" and "Real Love" were recorded onto tape cassette from a boom box. The tape cassettes of demos possessed all kinds of technical glitches and were crudely created.

On top of this was the heightened reality of fans clamoring for a Beatles reunion since their 1970 disbandment. Each solo member of the dissolved band was faced with the burdening hype of inquiries into a possible reunion. Paul, George, and Ringo quietly slipped into the studio and recorded two poignant songs left unfinished by John.

In essence, The Beatles made the impossible possible with their brief reunion. Both songs sounded fresh and inspiring. Taking those tattered cassette demos of their deceased friend, the reunited Beatles carved an audio miracle. Both songs were hits and received critical acclaim which culminated in Grammy Award recognition.

I was literally on the edge of my seat as I watched the countdown clock to "The Beatles Reunion" appear over the closing credits of Part 1 of ABC's "The Beatles Anthology." The video began for "Free as a Bird" and my heart soared. Hearing Paul's solo vocal turn during that song sealed it for me that I was in the middle of a Beatles reunion. It was The Beatles as one would hear them in 1995, and it made so much sense to me.

After witnessing Beatles history, I could not sleep. It was a school night and a full day of teaching was awaiting me. My eighth-grade students, who had put up with and encouraged my Beatles obsession, eagerly awaited my reaction to the new song. Their genuine and sincere support of my passion led me to integrate a formal lesson based on the music of The Beatles into my English-Language Arts class. I had played various songs for The Beatles as background music for various activities, but I had never officially taught them.

The reunion of The Beatles compelled me to tune in to enough courage to introduce their music within a planned lesson. I figured that "She's Leaving Home" from *Sgt. Pepper* was a logical place to introduce our upcoming poetry unit. What followed was an enriching jaunt into creativity with the class. Students connected with the heart-wrenching story of a teenage runaway as detailed by Lennon and McCartney's sharp lyrics and string-laded orchestration. Students collaborated in small groups to create an artistic interpretation of the song. I allowed their collective voices to take the song to new creative heights. My passion for music and their desire to explore the song further led me to go off my planned scripted lesson. Student voice conquered the constraints of the classroom, and a new level of expression ensued. Students produced a range of original artwork, mix tapes, storyboard renderings, and newscasts all based on extending their interpretation of the song. I simply stated for students to explore and interpret the song as they wanted to, without limits.

This was The Pepper Effect in full bloom in the classroom. I believed in a vision for my students to do something creative with music and literature. I knew that my class was going to create a plethora of masterpieces with this particular activity. This was not going to be a mere enrichment assignment—we were going to change the world with a masterpiece! I viewed my students as collaborators, and I believed in their inherent worth to take bold, giant steps as creative thinkers. We were so immersed in the creative pursuit and enjoying the process that there was no time to acknowledge the eye rolls at what could be perceived as a waste of instructional time.

> I believed in their inherent worth to take bold, giant steps as creative thinkers.

The template for this activity fueled my inspiration to integrate each moment in the classroom with meaning, relevance, and creativity for my students. I never let a day pass in the classroom without tuning in to their creativity. Some days were successful, and others were tremendous failures, but I had the picture of the reunited Beatles taped to my desk as a reminder that the impossible does become possible.

For our noble profession as educators, the impossible is a constant in the schoolhouse. We are bombarded with daunting odds, no-win scenarios, and decaying perceptions of our work. Varying labels are affixed to schools in an attempt to define a schoolwide achievement grade or solidify a false negative perception. I dream of a perfect shield to protect us all from our collective schoolwide challenges. There are various movements out there to support and uplift the beautiful work we do in service and support of our kids in the schoolhouse.

Sometimes there are days when those various positive movements are not enough to sustain me along the journey. Negativity drowns my vision, and I allow the echoes of naysayers to resonate. As a principal now, there are greater hurdles to overcome amidst seemingly impossible odds. A steady drumbeat of "These kids can't!" and "If only we had Program X to save us!" lifts the cacophony to Wagnerian volumes.

Despair is an easy fix.

Then I gaze at the tattered picture of a Beatles reunion.

The impossible became possible then.

I look back over past blessings and victories in the schoolhouse. I see a classroom transformed into a collaborative hub of creativity by a sad Beatles song. I see a young teacher getting his classroom confidence. I see schools transformed by dreams.

And I am "Free as a Bird."

Sgt. Pepper's Inner Groove: Tuning in to the Random, Eclectic, Whimsical Moments

CHAPTER 8

The Child is the father of the Man;

And I could wish my days to be

Bound each to each by natural piety.

—from "My Heart Leaps Up"
by William Wordsworth (1807)

———— SIDE 1 ————

Let's think outside the box for a moment or two.

Imagine reading this book in your hands. (Of course, I am grateful for your choice, and I appreciate you spending time with my words.)

Turn to the last page of the book. (Trust me, it will not spoil the ending. You will be fine, and I will not let anything happen to you.)

What if, as you finished reading the last page, there was a mechanism in this book that automatically forced you to return to the first page of the book? There you are on the last page of *The Pepper Effect*, and it won't let you finish. You try to let go, but your grip only tightens. The only way to escape is to place the book down on the nearest table.

There! You are free.

This is a silly hypothetical, a random and fantasy-filled notion, but the concept of doing something whimsical is something most of us can relate to. It's certainly evident on the final seconds of *Sgt. Pepper*. Following the apocalyptic ending of the album's final song, "A Day in the Life" (depending on which album version you own), The Beatles and some of their associates break out into a spontaneous cacophony of gibberish.

I first heard this snippet on the now out-of-print compilation, *The Beatles Rarities*. These two seconds are labeled on that particular album as "Sgt. Pepper Inner Groove." There was a rather mischievous intention behind this gibberish. If you had a record player in 1967 without an automatic stylus, the needle would play infinitely until you had to manually remove it from the record. The two-second gibberish on *Sgt. Pepper* could conceivably play for eternity on a non-automated record player.

As a kid, I would place my ear up to my little cassette player speaker (I had the tape version) and try to figure what nuttiness was being said. I could never figure it out, but I always enjoyed that snippet after the resonating crescendo of "A Day in the Life." It was the audio equivalent of a breath of fresh air. (Side note: The Beatles added a dog whistle as well at the end of the album. Only your friendly neighborhood canines can hear that whistle, but that's another story for another time.)

──── SIDE 2 ────

The "Sgt. Pepper Inner Groove" mishmash following "A Day in the Life" is a powerful reminder and fascinating contrast to explore. The Beatles were very aware that they were creating a masterpiece with this particular album. The album was a calculated risk recorded by a band wanting to push the boundaries of musical expression. It is filled with experimental sounds, avant-garde flavorings, Eastern-tinged instrumentation, orchestral flourishes, and poetic lyrics. I always thought this particular gibberish was a reminder by the band not to take oneself seriously. It is as if The Beatles are saying, "Yeah, we made this grand artistic statement, but we are still a bunch of blokes from Liverpool."

The brief blast of Jabberwocky sounds childlike and, in a way, connects back to the original concept for *Sgt. Pepper.*

Two of the greatest songs recorded by The Beatles—"Strawberry Fields Forever" and "Penny Lane"—were originally intended for that album. They were tracks based on real-life places in John Lennon's and Paul McCartney's native Liverpool. Both songs were written for an album that was originally intended to be a celebration of the band's childhood past. It is interesting to note that these songs rooted in nostalgic retrospection are two of the most progressive and innovative pieces of music The Beatles recorded. The concept of an album as an ode to their Liverpudlian childhood stalled when the record company needed songs for the then-popular singles market and radio airplay.

Childhood nostalgia is the fuel for some of the great works of art, music, film, and literature. As a former English teacher, I loved bringing in a song like "Penny Lane" to reinforce the beauty of nostalgia in a poem like "Fern Hill" by Dylan Thomas.

Our noble profession as educators is filled with moments of bliss, challenge, and grit. The schoolhouse is a place where childhood intersects with standards, compliance, and policies. Sometimes we default to rigidity rather than valuing what we are called as educators to do. The call is rooted in a support of the social and emotional well-being of the whole child. As an educator, I know all too well the realities burdening our noble profession. I am not calling for us to stop the bell schedule for a collective cry of gibberish like The Beatles did with "Sgt. Pepper Inner Groove"; however, perhaps we do need to tune in to our own inner groove as we support and serve our students.

Collaborating with students and supporting their creative voices is a step towards tuning in to that "Inner Groove." Celebrating Monday (#CelebrateMonday), committing random acts of kindness, and exploring in a makerspace are ways to promote the whole child by establishing a culture that is positive and inviting. These examples are planned with consideration for the unique needs and extraordinary gifts of our children. We have been entrusted, as educators, with the center of someone's universe. We must not forget that our students bring inspiring wonder and gifts to our respective schoolhouse communities.

> We have been entrusted, as educators, with the center of someone's universe.

It might be a fresh change of pace to simply divert from the grind of a scheduled activity in the schoolhouse. A whimsical diversion can fuel imagination, fun, and community.

When I first became principal at Lexington Middle School, I decided to pursue this whimsy with a classic childhood game. I wanted to find an introductory hook to build relationships, trust, and history with my new students in a positive way. I wanted to do something fun and easy that would help build towards the positive journey we were to experience in the schoolhouse. Again,

I was looking for a way to shed the paradigm of the typical principal. I yearned for a connection to show that I truly cared and that I wanted to be the president of the "student fan club" in our schoolhouse. My mind was struggling with this, perhaps because I knew first impressions are lasting. This is especially true in my role as a principal. I did not want to be viewed as some sort of villain.

I was visiting a class one day, getting myself acquainted with my new surroundings. I found an empty desk next to a student. I introduced myself. Admittedly, it was a little awkward. Here was the new principal crashing the classroom. I could tell that my presence was making the teacher a little nervous. Whispers and stares then followed. I could feel the sentiment of "Who's this guy?" emanating from those said whispers and stares.

My student companion adjacent to my desk provided a blank stare. I impulsively decided to introduce myself with the following question:

"Rock, Paper, and Scissors? You in?"

I formed my hands into Rock-Paper-Scissors stance. My challenge was accepted. We played a quick and quiet game. The ice was broken, and a relationship was established. Another student whispered to me, "I got you after class."

What evolved was a new tradition at Lexington Middle School. Any time I am in the hallways, cafeteria, bus lot, or classroom, I am happily challenged to a game of "Rock-Paper-Scissors." Students gather around, and we connect and have fun at the same time. Sometimes it makes me late for a meeting or conference, but it is truly worth it. Any kind of moment spent with students in a whimsical way is a worthwhile pursuit.

Part of me thinks a band that appreciated the absurd comedy of The Marx Brothers and Peter Sellers would approve of a random game of Rock-Paper-Scissors between students and a principal.

I imagine The Beatles nodding in approval and sending me wittily laced thumbs-up across the hallway.

Tapping into the nostalgia of childhood helped to fuel a world-changing album like *Sgt. Pepper* by The Beatles. Following along the Inner Groove of our childhood as educators can spark waves of creative possibility in the schoolhouse.

Your students and colleagues are waiting for your invitation to embrace the whimsical.

It's your move!

_____ MAKING YOUR MIX TAPE FOR _____ NEXT MOVES AND GROOVES:

Kids need that type of escape. It is a necessary ingredient for childhood imagination to take flight. We sometimes forget the fact that the very people at the center of our profession are children. They thrive on the freedom that imagination provides. It is our moral imperative as educators to provide an open and inviting doorway. There are many ways to do just that:

- Flip your classroom into an Escape Room designed by students.

- Have students send random notes of kindness to school community members.

- Take a walk around campus.

- Or . . . just ask your students! Their collective voice will inspire and lead down many good paths if simply asked and invited to do so.

The same can apply to other educator colleagues in the building. Take a random break from the scheduled tasks and reimagine the day with activities like...

- A flash-mob-style dance during a faculty meeting

- Random phone calls home to colleagues' family members, bragging on their achievements

- A coloring book party during a PLC meeting

- A rock-paper-scissors tournament

CHAPTER 9

"All You Need Is Love": In Service and Support of All Kids and Teachers

—— SIDE 1 ——

The closest I came to meeting one of The Beatles was at a Paul McCartney concert in Washington, DC several years ago.

A dream came true when my wife and I decided to take our three daughters to see the voice that had played incessantly in our household. Our children were exposed to viewings of Beatle films, such as *Yellow Submarine* and *A Hard Day's Night* and impromptu dance parties on the kitchen floor to the strains of "I Saw Her Standing There" and "Day Tripper." When our kids were newborns, I hummed the soft, meditative tones of "Across the Universe" and "Strawberry Fields Forever," and my wife always had "Imagine" at the ready to chase away their bad dreams.

The day of the concert, we had endured a long day of summer traffic, rushed Metro transfers, and crowds of tourists. As we stood waiting behind National Stadium, I noticed a large crowd of super fans huddled near a service entrance, and I mentioned we might get lucky and see Sir Paul drive by.

He did drive by and in the most unforgettable way.

As we stood on the street—the closest we could get to the entrance—a black SUV slowly pulled up alongside us, and a jovial face leaned out the passenger seat window. A harmonic "Wooo ..." was heard coming from the man who wrote "Yesterday," "Band on the Run," and "Hey Jude." In fact, it might have been in the same key as the "Wooo ..." on "Hey Jude."

I lost it, screaming at the top of my lungs, "It's Paul! It's Paul!" Yes, I proudly put those crazed female fans of the 1960s to shame. It was my own little Beatlemania meltdown—an eternal moment of a brush with a modern-day Beethoven that my family will always remember. I never met Paul McCartney, and he probably has no recollection of a semi-crazed, fortysomething-year-old family man jubilantly shouting upon his arrival. I am one of millions who have cherished his legacy.

Better than that is the moment I had with my eldest daughter later that night as he sang "All Together Now," one of our favorites from her preschool days. I have the moment with my twin daughters, recalling their memory of the loud fireworks erupting into the warm summer night during Paul's performance of "Live and Let Die."

I didn't meet The Beatles, but those moments with my daughters are better.

SIDE 2

Here's another one:

I was ten years old, my father had just been promoted, and our family had moved from California to the strange land of North Carolina. It was early in the school year, and I was reluctantly settling into St. Leo's Catholic School in Winston-Salem, North Carolina. One day I was walking into the school with my heavy backpack. I was dreading the day ahead, sure I would once again feel left out and bereft of any connection. As I walked, I was suddenly hit from behind. My fall to the ground generated much laughter as various books went flying out of my bag. A torrent of profanity flew from my frustrated lips.

As I fumbled to gather my belongings, a hand reached for my copy of *The Count of Monte Cristo*. It was Mrs. McMonagle, my fifth-grade teacher. She studied the book for a few moments before looking at me with a stark expression. Although barely five feet tall, her Scottish-British brogue could strike fear in all of us. Mrs. McMonagle slowly handed me the book. She asked me which reading group I was in. We had leveled reading groups in those days. Being in the lowest group, I always felt unchallenged and would look with envy at the accelerated group reading more interesting material.

Mrs. McMonagle's next words remain etched on my soul.

"What group are you in? Well, today join the 16A Group, and, Mr. Gaillard, you will need to watch your word choices. How about listening to something civilized and polite like The Beatles?"

It took one teacher to take the time to see something in me that no one else had. A journey began that day that led me down a beautiful path of learning, experiences, and connections. Mrs. McMonagle's support and belief in me served as the catalyst for my pursuit of teaching.

One teacher's words can set a life-changing course for a student to take bold, giant steps towards building a dynamic future.

Mrs. McMonagle's vision of a better world for students like me was similar to what The

One teacher's words can set a life-changing course for a student to take bold, giant steps towards building a dynamic future.

Beatles did as a band. They saw beyond themselves. Their list of failures is legendary. The Beatles were not highly regarded when they first started as a group of unlikely teenagers with a dream to be bigger than Elvis Presley. Name changes, unpaid gigs, drunken audience hecklers, and unstable line-ups are just some of the events that plagued the early days of The Beatles.

Despite all of the failure, ridicule, and doubt, the band persevered. They believed in themselves. Their manager and producer saw something in them and encouraged them to conquer new horizons as a band. As both musicians and collaborators, The Beatles saw something in each other that compelled them to strengthen their bond. This vision they had in each other as individuals formed a brotherhood that still inspires us today.

When The Beatles recorded *Sgt. Pepper* in the studio, I do not believe they were planning to change the world. The studio session outtakes and the banter between the band don't point to anything that prophetic or dramatic. It's simply four individuals with their producer and engineers taking an unabashed joy in the creative and collaborative process. The Beatles were following their various muses in a simple manner to create an album they knew would be bold and different.

They weren't taking themselves too seriously, because they wanted to avoid becoming a parody, and they were quick to mock the established and pretentious. In the end, they recorded a masterpiece, an album so innovative it recently re-entered the *Guinness Book of World Records* for the longest gap between appearances at number 1 on the British album charts.

All of these lessons from The Beatles can connect to the schoolhouse. The Beatles inspire and challenge us today with the bold experimentation of a conceptual album like *Sgt. Pepper*. We can do the same thing, as the schoolhouse is a musical work daring us to carve out new, fresh approaches to teaching and learning in an ever-shifting world.

Taking a page or two from The Beatles, a faculty can inspire and create and shift the paradigm of the schoolhouse into something that will stand the test of time for our students. As Steve Jobs said, "My model of business is The Beatles. They were four very talented guys who kept their negative tendencies relatively in check. They balanced each other, and the total was greater than the sum of its parts."

That sentiment applies to any school faculty. Fostering a culture of committed collaboration is a necessity. Students need our collective gifts harnessed at a high volume of collaboration. True collaboration breeds innovation. Again, think of The Beatles as a collective unit and the daring steps they undertook as a band. We would never have had a lasting work of art like *Sgt. Pepper* if The Beatles had been fragmented.

Schools cannot exist in isolation. Teachers and administrators cannot close their doors and scoff at the incorrectly perceived notion that collaboration is flash-in-the-pan fluff. We have to lean into each other and encourage each other to pick up our instruments and play our songs in unrelenting passion. This passion has to be rooted in service and support of those who dwell within the schoolhouse.

Adopting the ethos of The Pepper Effect can mean holding on to that innovative teacher looking for kindred bandmates to collaborate with or encouraging the student who is contemplating her dreams.

The Beatles embraced newness in their trajectory as a band. Finding original ways to express their

> We have to lean into each other and encourage each other to pick up our instruments and play our songs in unrelenting passion.

musical marrow, The Beatles never settled for the comfort of the status quo. They were very much aware of their audience and signs of the times.

After they established the quantum leap of the *Sgt. Pepper* album, The Beatles kept moving forward with their expedition of sound. Classic albums followed, which are now engraved within the eternity of recorded sound. Generations to come will discover the glorious sounds of this little pub band from Liverpool that made it very big.

Imagine the same mindset within education. What if educators approached the art and science of teaching with the same innovative abandon as The Beatles did when creating *Sgt. Pepper*?

What if educators embraced the same randomness The Beatles and Producer George Martin did when they tossed the calliope organ parts from "Being for the Benefit of Mr. Kite" up in the air and stitched them together without rhyme or reason to create a new sound?

What if we took a bold turn and integrated Indian orchestration, embracing global education on a song like "Within You Without You?"

What if we decided to take random observations from the newspaper and thread them into lyrics like in "She's Leaving Home," thus stretching our creative muscles?

What if we rallied around a bandmate, just as The Beatles did for Ringo, on a song like "With a Little Help from My Friends"? Imagine the strength emanating into a sustained bond of love and trust when educators truly forge collaboration like a band.

What if we adopted a new persona to reimagine our approach to tried instructional practices as The Beatles reinvented themselves into the Sgt. Pepper Band?

What if we connected with our kids as The Beatles did in wanting to create something bold and innovative for their fans? What if we created something every day at masterpiece levels for our kids? What if we inspired our kids to do the same thing?

Imagine the legacy of joy and positivity that lies ahead in the schoolhouse.

Embrace the quantum leap with your schoolhouse band and soar towards changing the world by playing your symphony.

The world awaits your positive impact!

Praise and Thanks!

- Praise and thanks for Deb, Maddie, Emily, and Rachel: You are my true Fab Four, and I will always be a proud husband and father. Someday we will cross Abbey Road together for that album-cover family pic I have always wanted.

- Praise and thanks for my Gaillard family for always believing in and supporting me! I am eternally grateful for the loving example of my parents. Special thanks to my big brother and little sisters for putting up with my incessant playing of The Beatles in our household.

- Praise and thanks for my teachers who have inspired me to be a better person for others: Mrs. Sandra McMonagle, my fifth-grade teacher, who taught me the art of writing and communication; Sister Janet Stolba, who taught me how to teach; Ms. Debbie Brooks, who taught me how to lead as a servant; Dr. Carol Montague-Davis, who taught me how to lead with compassion.

- Praise and thanks for the students, faculty, and families of Wiley Magnet Middle School, John F. Kennedy High School, and Lexington Middle School—thanks for changing my life and making our world a better place. I will always be the president of your fan club!

- Praise and thanks for Nicole Michael of 910 Public Relations for a conversation that sparked *The Pepper Effect* dream!

- Praise and thanks for lifelong friends Max Pizarro, Jennifer Williams, Doug Heye, and Jeff Howard for writing encouragement over the years!

- Praise and thanks for endorsements from my #EduHeroes: Todd Whitaker, Elisabeth Bostwick, Allyson Apsey, Jennifer Burdis, Marlena Gross-Taylor, Brad Spirrison, Megan Morgan, Kenneth Womack, Laura Fleming, Randy Ziegenfuss, Beth Houf, and Aaron Krerowicz.

- Thanks to Joey and Brook Cutts of Urban Bloom Photography!

- Thanks to Jennifer Williams for writing a beautiful foreword to this book! I am eternally grateful for her friendship and support.

- Special praise and thanks for Dave and Shelley Burgess for constant belief, support, and encouragement to pursue this book dream! I am eternally grateful for the two of them and their amazing team!

Bring Sean Gaillard
to Your School or District

Sean Gaillard loves to share the magic of collaboration and innovation with teachers and school leaders. His fun and engaging workshops and keynote sessions spark ideas and empower educators to find new, exciting grooves in their work. Sean wants to provide sincere support for educators seeking fresh ideas with building school culture and establishing collaborative teams. Gaillard's professional development presentations are tailored to inspire and motivate everyone involved to play together in the band.

Popular session topics include . . .

- #CelebrateMonday: Trending the Positive in Your School by Starting with One Day
- Make Your School a Masterpiece
- Vision Building
- Tap into the Magic of Collaboration

To learn more and to book Sean to speak
at an upcoming event, visit . . .

 principallinernotes.wordpress.com

 @smgaillard

 sgaillard84@gmail.com

More from

DAVE BURGESS
Consulting, Inc.

LEAD Like a PIRATE

Make School Amazing for Your Students and Staff

By Shelley Burgess and Beth Houf
(@Burgess_Shelley, @BethHouf)

Lead Like a PIRATE maps out character traits necessary to captain a school or district. You'll learn where to find treasure already in your classrooms and schools—and bring out the best in educators. Find encouragement in your relentless quest to make school amazing for everyone!

Lead with Culture

What Really Matters in Our Schools

By Jay Billy (@JayBilly2)

In this Lead Like a PIRATE Guide, Jay Billy explains that making school a place where students and staff want to be starts with culture. You'll be inspired by this principal's practical ideas for creating a sense of unity—even in the most diverse communities.

Teach Like a PIRATE

Increase Student Engagement, Boost Your Creativity, and Transform Your Life as an Educator

By Dave Burgess (@BurgessDave)

New York Times' bestseller Teach Like a PIRATE sparked a worldwide educational revolution with its passionate teaching manifesto and dynamic student-engagement strategies. Translated into multiple languages, it sparks outrageously creative lessons and life-changing student experiences.

Learn Like a PIRATE

Empower Your Students to Collaborate, Lead, and Succeed

By Paul Solarz (@PaulSolarz)

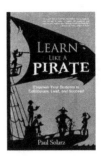

Passing grades don't equip students for life and career responsibilities. *Learn Like a PIRATE* shows how risk taking and exploring passions in stimulating, motivating, supportive, self-directed classrooms create students capable of making smart, responsible decisions on their own.

P is for PIRATE

Inspirational ABC's for Educators

By Dave and Shelley Burgess (@Burgess_Shelley)

In *P is for Pirate*, husband-and-wife team Dave and Shelley Burgess tap personal experiences of seventy educators to inspire others to create fun and exciting places to learn. It's a wealth of imaginative and creative ideas that make learning and teaching more fulfilling than ever before.

eXPlore Like a Pirate

Gamification and Game-Inspired Course Design to Engage, Enrich, and Elevate Your Learners

By Michael Matera (@MrMatera)

Create an experiential, collaborative, and creative world with classroom game designer and educator Michael Matera's game-based learning book, *eXPlore Like a Pirate*. Matera helps teachers apply motivational gameplay techniques and enhance curriculum with gamification strategies.

Play Like a Pirate

Engage Students with Toys, Games, and Comics

By Quinn Rollins (@jedikermit)

In *Play Like a Pirate*, Quinn Rollins offers practical, engaging strategies and resources that make it easy to integrate fun into your curriculum. Regardless of grade level, serious learning can be seriously fun with inspirational ideas that engage students in unforgettable ways.

The Innovator's Mindset

Empower Learning, Unleash Talent, and Lead a Culture of Creativity

By George Couros (@gcouros)

In *The Innovator's Mindset*, teachers and administrators discover that compliance to a scheduled curriculum hinders student innovation, critical thinking, and creativity. To become forward-thinking leaders, students must be empowered to wonder and explore.

Pure Genius

Building a Culture of Innovation and Taking 20% Time to the Next Level

By Don Wettrick (@DonWettrick)

Collaboration—with experts, students, and other educators—helps create interesting and even life-changing opportunities for learning. In *Pure Genius*, Don Wettrick inspires and equips educators with a systematic blueprint for beating classroom boredom and teaching innovation.

Ditch That Textbook

Free Your Teaching and Revolutionize Your Classroom

By Matt Miller (@jmattmiller)

Ditch That Textbook creates a support system, toolbox, and manifesto that can free teachers from outdated textbooks. Miller empowers them to untether themselves, throw out meaningless, pedestrian teaching and learning practices, and evolve and revolutionize their classrooms.

50 Things You Can Do with Google Classroom

By Alice Keeler and Libbi Miller
(@alicekeeler, @MillerLibbi)

50 Things You Can Do with Google Classroom provides a thorough overview of this GAfE app and shortens the teacher learning curve for introducing technology in the classroom. Keeler and Miller's ideas, instruction, and screenshots help teachers go digital with this powerful tool.

50 Things to Go Further with Google Classroom

A Student-Centered Approach

By Alice Keeler and Libbi Miller
(@alicekeeler, @MillerLibbi)

In *50 Things to Go Further with Google Classroom: A Student-Centered Approach*, authors and educators Alice Keeler and Libbi Miller help teachers create a digitally rich, engaging, student-centered environment that taps the power of individualized learning using Google Classroom.

140 Twitter Tips for Educators

Get Connected, Grow Your Professional Learning Network, and Reinvigorate Your Career

By Brad Currie, Billy Krakower, and Scott Rocco
(@bradmcurrie, @wkrakower, @ScottRRocco)

In *140 Twitter Tips for Educators*, #Satchat hosts and founders of Evolving Educators, Brad Currie, Billy Krakower, and Scott Rocco, offer step-by-step instruction on Twitter basics and building an online following within Twitter's vibrant network of educational professionals.

Master the Media

How Teaching Media Literacy Can Save Our Plugged-In World

By Julie Smith (@julnilsmith)

Master the Media explains media history, purpose, and messaging, so teachers and parents can empower students with critical-thinking skills, which lead to informed choices, the ability to differentiate between truth and lies, and discern perception from reality. Media literacy can save the world.

The Zen Teacher

Creating Focus, Simplicity, and Tranquility in the Classroom

By Dan Tricarico (@thezenteacher)

Unrushed and fully focused, teachers influence—even improve—the future when they maximize performance and improve their quality of life. In *The Zen Teacher*, Dan Tricarico offers practical, easy-to-use techniques to develop a non-religious Zen practice and thrive in the classroom.

Your School Rocks . . . So Tell People!

Passionately Pitch and Promote the Positives Happening on Your Campus

By Ryan McLane and Eric Lowe (@McLane_Ryan, @EricLowe21)

Your School Rocks . . . So Tell People! helps schools create effective social media communication strategies that keep students' families and the community connected to what's going on at school, offering more than seventy immediately actionable tips with easy-to-follow instructions and video tutorial links.

The Classroom Chef

Sharpen Your Lessons. Season Your Classes. Make Math Meaningful

By John Stevens and Matt Vaudrey
(@Jstevens009, @MrVaudrey)

With imagination and preparation, every teacher can be *The Classroom Chef* using John Stevens and Matt Vaudrey's secret recipes, ingredients, and tips that help students "get" math. Use ideas as-is, or tweak to create enticing educational meals that engage students.

How Much Water Do We Have?

5 Success Principles for Conquering Any Challenge and Thriving in Times of Change

By Pete Nunweiler with Kris Nunweiler

Stressed out, overwhelmed, or uncertain at work or home? It could be figurative dehydration.

How Much Water Do We Have? identifies five key elements necessary for success of any goal, life transition, or challenge. Learn to find, acquire, and use the 5 Waters of Success.

The Writing on the Classroom Wall

How Posting Your Most Passionate Beliefs about Education Can Empower Your Students, Propel Your Growth, and Lead to a Lifetime of Learning

By Steve Wyborney (@SteveWyborney)

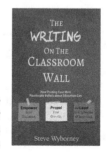

Big ideas lead to deeper learning, but they don't have to be profound to have profound impact. Teacher Steve Wyborney explains why and how sharing ideas sharpens and refines them. It's okay if some ideas fall off the wall; what matters most is sharing and discussing.

Kids Deserve It!

Pushing Boundaries and Challenging Conventional Thinking

By Todd Nesloney and Adam Welcome
(@TechNinjaTodd, @awelcome)

Think big. Make learning fun and meaningful. *Kids Deserve It!* Nesloney and Welcome offer high-tech, high-touch, and highly engaging practices that inspire risk taking and shake up the status quo on behalf of your students. Rediscover why you became an educator, too!

LAUNCH

Using Design Thinking to Boost Creativity and Bring Out the Maker in Every Student

By John Spencer and A.J. Juliani (@spencerideas, @ajjuliani)

When students identify themselves as makers, inventors, and creators, they discover powerful problem-solving and critical-thinking skills. Their imaginations and creativity will shape our future. John Spencer and A.J. Juliani's *LAUNCH* process dares you to innovate and empower them.

Instant Relevance

Using Today's Experiences to Teach Tomorrow's Lessons

By Denis Sheeran (@MathDenisNJ)

Learning sticks when it's relevant to students. In *Instant Relevance,* author and keynote speaker Denis Sheeran equips you to create engaging lessons *from* experiences and events that matter to students while helping them make meaningful connections between the real world and the classroom.

Escaping the School Leader's Dunk Tank

How to Prevail When Others Want to See You Drown

By Rebecca Coda and Rick Jetter
(@RebeccaCoda, @RickJetter)

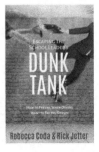

Dunk-tank situations—discrimination, bad politics, revenge, or ego-driven coworkers—can make an educator's life miserable. Coda and Jetter (dunk-tank survivors themselves) share real-life stories and insightful research to equip school leaders with tools to survive and, better yet, avoid getting "dunked."

Start. Right. Now.

Teach and Lead for Excellence

By Todd Whitaker, Jeff Zoul, and Jimmy Casas
(@ToddWhitaker, @Jeff_Zoul, @casas_jimmy)

Excellent leaders and teachers *Know the Way, Show the Way, Go the Way, and Grow Each Day*. Whitaker, Zoul, and Casas share four key behaviors of excellence from educators across the U.S. and motivate to put you on the right path.

Teaching Math with Google Apps

50 G Suite Activities

By Alice Keeler and Diana Herrington

(@AliceKeeler, @mathdiana)

Teaching Math with Google Apps meshes the easy student/teacher interaction of Google Apps with G Suite that empowers student creativity and critical thinking. Keeler and Herrington demonstrate fifty ways to bring math classes into the twenty-first century with easy-to-use technology.

Table Talk Math

A Practical Guide for Bringing Math into Everyday Conversations

By John Stevens (@Jstevens009)

In *Table Talk Math,* John Stevens offers parents—and teachers—ideas for initiating authentic, math-based, everyday conversations that get kids to notice and pique their curiosity about the numbers, patterns, and equations in the world around them.

Shift This!

How to Implement Gradual Change for Massive Impact in Your Classroom

By Joy Kirr (@JoyKirr)

Establishing a student-led culture focused on individual responsibility and personalized learning *is* possible, sustainable, and even easy when it happens little by little. In *Shift This!,* Joy Kirr details gradual shifts in thinking, teaching, and approach for massive impact in your classroom.

Unmapped Potential

An Educator's Guide to Lasting Change

By Julie Hasson and Missy Lennard (@PPrincipals)

Overwhelmed and overworked? You're not alone, but it can get better. You simply need the right map to guide you from frustrated to fulfilled. *Unmapped Potential* offers advice and practical strategies to forge a unique path to becoming the educator and *person* you want to be.

Shattering the Perfect Teacher Myth

6 Truths That Will Help You THRIVE as an Educator

By Aaron Hogan (@aaron_hogan)

Author and educator Aaron Hogan helps shatter the idyllic "perfect teacher" myth, which erodes self-confidence with unrealistic expectations and sets teachers up for failure. His book equips educators with strategies that help them shift out of survival mode and THRIVE.

Social LEADia

Moving Students from Digital Citizenship to Digital Leadership

By Jennifer Casa-Todd (@JCasaTodd)

A networked society requires students to leverage social media to connect to people, passions, and opportunities to grow and make a difference. *Social LEADia* helps shift focus at school and home from digital citizenship to digital leadership and equip students for the future.

Spark Learning

3 Keys to Embracing the Power of Student Curiosity

By Ramsey Musallam (@ramusallam)

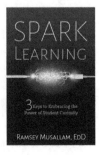

Inspired by his popular TED Talk "3 Rules to Spark Learning," Musallam combines brain science research, proven teaching methods, and his personal story to empower you to improve your students' learning experiences by inspiring inquiry and harnessing its benefits.

Ditch That Homework

Practical Strategies to Help Make Homework Obsolete

By Matt Miller and Alice Keeler (@jmattmiller, @alicekeeler)

In *Ditch That Homework*, Miller and Keeler discuss the pros and cons of homework, why it's assigned, and what life could look like without it. They evaluate research, share parent and teacher insights, then make a convincing case for ditching it for effective and personalized learning methods.

The Four O'Clock Faculty

A Rogue Guide to Revolutionizing Professional Development

By Rich Czyz (@RACzyz)

In *The Four O'Clock Faculty*, Rich identifies ways to make professional learning meaningful, efficient, and, above all, personally relevant. It's a practical guide to revolutionize PD, revealing why some is so awful and what *you* can do to change the model for the betterment of everyone.

Culturize

Every Student. Every Day. Whatever It Takes.

By Jimmy Casas (@casas_jimmy)

Culturize dives into what it takes to cultivate a community of learners who embody innately human traits our world desperately needs—kindness, honesty, and compassion. Casas's stories reveal how "soft skills" can be honed while exceeding academic standards of twenty-first-century learning.

Code Breaker

Increase Creativity, Remix Assessment, and Develop a Class of Coder Ninjas!

By Brian Aspinall (@mraspinall)

You don't have to be a "computer geek" to use coding to turn curriculum expectations into student skills. Use *Code Breaker* to teach students how to identify problems, develop solutions, and use computational thinking to apply and demonstrate learning.

The Wild Card

7 Steps to an Educator's Creative Breakthrough

By Hope and Wade King (@hopekingteach, @wadeking7)

The Kings facilitate a creative breakthrough in the classroom with *The Wild Card*, a step-by-step guide to drawing on your authentic self to deliver your content creatively and be the *wild card* who changes the game for your learners.

Stories from Webb

The Ideas, Passions, and Convictions of a Principal and His School Family

By Todd Nesloney (@TechNinjaTodd)

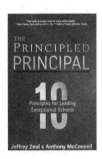

Stories from Webb goes right to the heart of education. Told by award-winning principal Todd Nesloney and his dedicated team of staff and teachers, this book reminds you why you became an educator. Relatable stories reinvigorate and may inspire you to tell your own!

The Principled Principal

10 Principles for Leading Exceptional Schools

By Jeffrey Zoul and Anthony McConnell (@Jeff_Zoul, @mcconnellaw)

Zoul and McConnell know from personal experience that the role of a school principal is one of the most challenging *and* the most rewarding in education. Using relatable stories and real-life examples, they reveal ten core values that will empower you to work and lead with excellence.

The Limitless School

Creative Ways to Solve the Culture Puzzle

By Abe Hege and Adam Dovico (@abehege, @adamdovico)

Being intentional about creating a positive culture is imperative for your school's success. This book identifies the nine pillars that support a positive school culture and explains how each stakeholder has a vital role to play in the work of making schools safe, inviting, and dynamic.

Google Apps for Littles

Believe They Can

By Christine Pinto and Alice Keeler
(@PintoBeanz11, @alicekeeler)

Learn how to tap into students' natural curiosity using technology. Pinto and Keeler share a wealth of innovative ways to integrate digital tools in the primary classroom to make learning engaging and relevant for even the youngest of today's twenty-first-century learners.

Be the One for Kids

You Have the Power to Change the Life of a Child

By Ryan Sheehy (@sheehyrw)

Students need guidance to succeed academically, but they also need our help to survive and thrive in today's turbulent world. They need someone to model the attributes that will help them win not just in school but in life as well. That someone is you.

Let Them Speak

How Student Voice Can Transform Your School

By Rebecca Coda and Rick Jetter
(@RebeccaCoda, @RickJetter)

We say, "Student voice matters," but are we really listening? This book will inspire you to find out what your students really think, feel, and need. You'll learn how to listen to and use student feedback to improve your school's culture. All you have to do is ask—and then *Let Them Speak*.

The EduProtocol Field Guide

16 Student-Centered Lesson Frames for Infinite Learning Possibilities

By Marlena Hebren and Jon Corippo

Are you ready to break out of the lesson-and-worksheet rut? Use *The EduProtocol Field Guide* to create engaging and effective instruction, build culture, and deliver content to K–12 students in a supportive, creative environment.

All 4s and 5s

A Guide to Teaching and Leading Advanced Placement Programs

By Andrew Sharos

AP classes shouldn't be relegated to "privileged" schools and students. With proper support, every student can experience success. *All 4s and 5s* offers a wealth of classroom and program strategies that equip you to develop a culture of academic and personal excellence.

Shake Up Learning

Practical Ideas to Move Learning from Static to Dynamic

By Kasey Bell (@ShakeUpLearning)

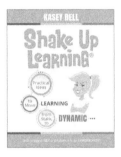

Is the learning in your classroom static or dynamic? *Shake Up Learning* guides you through the process of creating dynamic learning opportunities—from purposeful planning and maximizing technology to fearless implementation.

The Secret Solution

How One Principal Discovered the Path to Success

Todd Whitaker, Sam Miller, and Ryan Donlan
(@ToddWhitaker, @SamMiller29, @RyanDonlan)

An entertaining look at the path to leadership excellence, this parable provides leaders with a non-threatening tool to discuss problematic attitudes in schools. This updated edition includes a reader's guide to help you identify habits and traits that can help you and your team succeed.

The Path to Serendipity

Discover the Gifts along Life's Journey

By Allyson Apsey (@AllysonApsey)

In this funny, genuine, and clever book, Allyson Apsey shares relatable stories and practical strategies for living a meaningful life regardless of the craziness happening around you. You'll discover that you really do have the power to choose the kind of life you live—every day.

The EduNinja Mindset

11 Habits for Building a Stronger Mind and Body

By Jennifer Burdis (@jennifer_burdis)

As a two-time *American Ninja Warrior* contestant, educator, and trainer, Jen Burdis pushes herself to physically and mentally overcome obstacles. In *The EduNinja Mindset*, Burdis shares her strategies to empower teachers, students and fami-lies to develop healthy habits.

About the Author

Sean Gaillard has more than twenty years of experience in education as a teacher and school administrator. He is currently principal at Lexington Middle School in Lexington, North Carolina. Prior to that role, Sean served as principal at Wiley Magnet Middle School and John F. Kennedy High School, both located in Winston-Salem, North Carolina.

Sean has contributed various writings for *Education Week*, "PBS News Hour Extra," and "Education Closet." His contributions have been featured in various books on school leadership and music. Sean's writings are featured on his blog, *Principal Liner Notes*. He is passionate about school culture, innovation, and all things music.

Sean founded the Twitter hashtag, #CelebrateMonday, a school culture movement that celebrates positivity in the schoolhouse. He has presented at various conferences including ISTE and the National School Board Association Conference. When he is not in the schoolhouse or browsing in used record stores, Sean lives with his real Fab Four: Deborah (his wife) and their three daughters.